Insurance Law in Italy

Insurance Law in Italy

Diana Cerini

This book was originally published as a monograph in the International Encyclopaedia of Laws/Insurance Law.

General Editor: Roger Blanpain
Associate General Editor: Michele Colucci
Volume Editor: Herman Cousy

Wolters Kluwer
Law & Business

Published by:
Kluwer Law International
PO Box 316
2400 AH Alphen aan den Rijn
The Netherlands
Website: www.kluwerlaw.com

Sold and distributed in North, Central and South America by:
Aspen Publishers, Inc.
7201 McKinney Circle
Frederick, MD 21704
United States of America
Email: customer.service@aspenpublishers.com

Sold and distributed in all other countries by:
Turpin Distribution Services Ltd.
Stratton Business Park
Pegasus Drive, Biggleswade
Bedfordshire SG18 8TQ
United Kingdom
Email: kluwerlaw@turpin-distribution.com

DISCLAIMER: The material in this volume is in the nature of general comment only. It is not offered as advice on any particular matter and should not be taken as such. The editor and the contributing authors expressly disclaim all liability to any person with regard to anything done or omitted to be done, and with respect to the consequences of anything done or omitted to be done wholly or partly in reliance upon the whole or any part of the contents of this volume. No reader should act or refrain from acting on the basis of any matter contained in this volume without first obtaining professional advice regarding the particular facts and circumstances at issue. Any and all opinions expressed herein are those of the particular author and are not necessarily those of the editor or publisher of this volume.

Printed on acid-free paper.

ISBN 978-90-411-4575-8

This title is available on www.kluwerlawonline.com

Printed and Bound by CPI Group (UK) Ltd, Croydon, CR0 4YY.

The Author

Diana Cerini is a lawyer and associate professor in Comparative Law at the Law Faculty of Università Statale di Milano-Bicocca; she is also Professor in Insurance Law for the Master Programme (MAPA) at LIUC University of Castellanza. She has extensive experience in international research on comparative law and in insurance law specifically. She is member for Italy of the European Project Group for the Restatement of Insurance Contract Law.

She has authored several books and papers on insurance and tort law subjects.

The Author

4

Table of Contents

Table of Contents

Table of Contents

Table of Contents

Table of Contents

Table of Contents

Table of Contents

List of Abbreviations

Laws and Regulations

CC	*Codice Civile (Civil Code)*
CAP	*Codice delle Assicurazioni Private (Code of Private* Insurances)
C Cons.	*Codice del Consumo (Consumer Code)*
CP	*Codice Penale (Criminal Code)*
TUIR	*Testo Unico Imposta sui Redditi (Tax Law)*
TUF	*Testo Unico Intermediazione Finanziaria (Finance* Law)
DPR	*Decreto Presidente Repubblica (Decree by the Presi*dent of the Italian Republic)
L.	*Legge (Law)*
D.Lgs or	
LGS. D.	*Decreto Legislativo (Legislative Decree)* Law Reviews
Ass.	*Assicurazioni (Insurances)*
DEA	*Diritto ed economia dell'assicurazione (Law and* economics of insurance)
DT	*Diritto dei trasporti (Transport law)*
EGI	*Enciclopedia Giuridica Italiana (Italian Law* *Encyclo*paedia)
FI (or Foro It. – both used)	*Foro Italiano*
GC, Mass	*Giurisprudenza Civile, Mass (Civil Law cases)*
Giur. mer.	*Giurisprudenza di Merito (Case Law Review)*
Giust. Civ.	*Giustizia Civile (Civil Justice Law Review)*
NGC	*Nuova Giurisprudenza Civile (New Civil Justice Law* Review)
Other Abbreviations	
ISVAP	*Istituto di vigilanza sulle assicurazioni private* (Supervisory authority for insurance)
COVIP	*Commissione di vigilanza sui fondi pensione (Super*visory authority for pension funds)
ANIA	*Associazione nazionale imprese assicuratrici (National* Association of Insurance Companies)

List of Abbreviations

Cass.	(decision of) Corte di Cassazione – Court of Cassation or Supreme Court
Cass. civ.	(decision of) Corte di Cassazione, civil section
Corte App.	(decision of) Corte d'Appello (Court of Appeal)
TAR	(decision of) Tribunale Amministrativo Regionale (Regional Administrative Court)
Trib.	*Tribunale (ordinary civil court – first degree)*

Preliminary Notes

The present volume on Italian insurance law aims at being a useful and practical tool in the hands of those interested in discovering the Italian landscape of insurance law.

After years of debates and months of work, the Legislative Decree No. 209 of 7 September 2005, published in the GU No. 239 of 13 October 2005 and titled *Decreto legislativo recante riassetto normativo delle disposizioni in materia di assicurazione private – also called Codice delle Assicurazioni Private or 'CAP'* was approved and it entered into force on 1 January 2006.

The *Codice delle Assicurazioni Private* replaces, in large part, and complements the whole legislative regulation on the subject of insurance. The rules covered by the Civil Code concerning the insurance contract are preserved, and the new rules have to be coordinated with them. Moreover, the Code provides for the approval of executive rules and regulations by ISVAP, that is to say the Italian Control Authority on Private Insurance; since now, thirty-nine regulations have been approved (they are all available on the website www.isvap.it). The abrogation of old rules is not necessarily coincident with the date of effect of the Code but is submitted to the progressive approval of the said executive rules. In other words, the rescinding of the actual legislation has to be determined in the relevant case according to the date when the executive rules are approved: after five years, some provisions are still missing as even if the work already done by the Control Authority is remarkable.

In this light, it is clear why the current regulatory framework looks somewhat confused and problematic for internal operators as well as for the foreign observers. For this reason, from an operative point of view, it seems appropriate to provide the reader with both the reference and numeration of the current legislation or regulation (or even Circular Letter by the Authority) that is still in force and the reference and enumeration adopted in the *Codice delle Assicurazioni Private* (CAP). Where the new rule modifies the old one in its content and not only in its formal reference, the reader will be advised.

Diana Cerini

Preliminary Notes

General Introduction

Chapter 1. The Italian Political System and State Organization

1. According to our Constitution, Italy is a democratic Republic founded on work and solidarity. The history that leads to the actual situation has been long and tortuous, requiring the unification of the territory, in first place, and then the transition from the monarchy to the republic. The legal history of the country is strictly linked to the historical steps that lead to the actual republic.

In fact, the unity of Italy was reached in 1861; the United Kingdom of Italy was proclaimed in 1865. After the proclaiming of the United Kingdom of Italy, the Italian Parliament approved a Civil Code and a few years later (1882) a Commercial Code. The approval of the Codes was intended as an important symbol of the United Kingdom and of the independence of the country from foreign influences, even if the distinction between the civil and commercial code is debtor to the French solution.

During the Fascist period Italian democracy was in abeyance. This period ended after the Second World War, with the transformation of the kingdom into the Italian Democratic Republic. On 25 June 1944, a decree was enacted by the government calling for the election of a constitutional assembly with the power to approve the Republican Constitution. This Constitution was finally approved on 22 December 1947 and enacted on 1 January 1948.

2. The Republican Constitution establishes the balance of the powers of the state. According to the Constitution (Articles 55–70), legislative power is conferred on Parliament which is formed of two different chambers: the *Camera dei Deputati* (Chamber of deputies) and the *Senato* (Senate). Executive power is conferred on the *Governo* (government), which is comprised of the Prime Minister and his/her ministers (Article 92 Constitution). The judiciary power is vested in the courts. The judiciary power is proclaimed to be completely independent (Article 102 Constitution).

Chapter 2. The Italian Legal System and Sources of Law

3. Italy is a civil law country, even better described as the cradle of European legal culture.[1] The origin of the Italian legal system dates back to the Roman Empire. First developed in the ancient world, Roman law had a strong impact on the present legal system as, after the fall of the Roman Empire and the era of the *ius commune*, did the French model (mainly in the nineteenth century) and later the German (second half of the twentieth century) and the common law models (in the final decades of the previous century).

As in the majority of the European legal systems, Italian law was marked by a period of codification (nineteenth century). This period left some basic elements of legal thought such as the division of powers and the superiority of formal law over other legal sources.

4. The actual sources of Italian law cannot be traced to the Republican Constitution except in their most general design. In fact, the Constitution only describes the organization of the Republic and the role of the legislative, governmental and judiciary powers,[2] clarifying that Parliament is vested with legislative power which is to be exercised by the two chambers together.

The actual structure of the sources of law is instead to be found in Article 1 of the 'Provisions on the Law in general' (also called *Preleggi*) which were approved together with the Civil Code of 4 April 1942, replacing the previous code of 1865.

Article 1 enumerates the following sources of law: national ordinary statutes (or ordinary laws), administrative regulations, corporate regulations and customs.

This enumeration reflects a hierarchy whereby the latter cannot take precedence over the former.

This hierarchy of law described in the Provisions on the Law in general is in fact very incomplete and has been profoundly changed during the last sixty years even though Article 1 has not formally been modified. In fact, the hierarchy of the sources of law has to be combined with the modifications in the social and legislative structure that have taken place since 1942.

As a consequence, the Republican Constitution approved in 1947 currently stands at the top of the hierarchy of laws. It can therefore be amended only by a special procedure provided for in Article 138 of the Constitution itself.

Immediately below the Constitution are *leggi ordinarie*, that is to say national ordinary laws approved by Parliament. The Civil Code of 1942, which is the fundamental text for private law, was approved in the form of an ordinary law. In addition there exists a large number of ordinary laws collateral to the civil codification.

At the same level of ordinary laws stand Acts that are approved by the government but are endowed with the value of ordinary laws: these are the so-called *decreti legge* (law decrees) and *decreti legislativi* (legislative decrees).

---

1. See A. Cannata & A. Gambaro, Lineamenti di Storia della giurisprudenza europea, Turin, 1984; A. Padoa Schioppa,'A sketch of legal history', in Introduction to *Italian Law* ,ed. J.S. Lena & U. Mattei (Kluwer, 2002), 1ff; T.G. Watkin, The Italian Legal Tradition, Ashgate, 1997, 1.
2. For a wider description see M. Comba, in *Introduction to Italian law*, ed. Jeffrey S. Lena & U. Mattei, (Kluwer, 2002), 31ff. and see the selected bibliography.

In a complementary position to national laws stand the regional statutes that prevail with respect to specific subject matter.

5.   In the third place of the hierarchy stand administrative regulations. These acts are normative measures taken by the executive power to regulate specific activities. Minor public entities have comparable competence but the precise force of the acts that they promulgate is not always clear.

6.   The hierarchy of laws would not be complete if international sources of law were not mentioned. In fact, according to Article 10 of the Constitution, Italy's legal system 'respects the generally accepted and recognized principles and customs of international law'. As a consequence, the general principles and customs are automatically part of the Italian legal system.

By virtue of Article 10 of the Constitution Italy also accepts a limitation of its sovereignty by virtue of international treaties. As a consequence European Community law prevails over domestic law.

7.   In the Italian legal system, the decisions of the judiciary courts are not considered as sources of the law, although they have a strong impact on future laws and decisions. Judicial decisions are only binding on the parties. However, decisions by the Supreme Court have an important and strong persuasive effect.

Chapter 3. History and Sources of Insurance Law

8. The roots of the insurance business are centuries old. Their origins are said to be Italian. While incorporating the heritage of activities performed by ancient mutual societies, modern insurance as a technique for transferring and spreading risk was created by Italian merchants in the fourteenth century in relation to maritime risks.

Because of its commercial origins, for a long period the insurance business was subject only to commercial usages and to specific local statutes the aim of which was of a public law nature rather than to regulate the contractual relation between the parties. In fact the goals of these statutes were comparable to the laws that prohibited usury, games and gambling.

Later on (in the fifteenth century) a number of statutes concerning the contract were enacted especially thanks to the influence of the French legislation.

Terrestrial 'non-marine' insurance contracts appeared in the seventeenth century. The first insurance policies covered damage to property and it was only some decades later that life insurance came about. In the eighteenth and nineteenth centuries new rules appeared and were finally collected in the Commercial Code of 1882. The rules it contained were mostly default rules and were applied, with a few exceptions, only in the case of lack of discipline by the parties.[3]

9. As a consequence of political changes and historic events, the present sources of Italian insurance law are quite varied, both in their origin and in their form. In fact, the rules concerning the insurance contract are mainly included in the Civil Code of 1942, which introduced substantial changes to the system of the Commercial Code after its abrogation. This was the occasion not only for modifying a number of rules, but mainly for introducing the mandatory character of many provisions.

In order to have a comprehensive view of the body of rules applicable to insurance contract, not only the rules concerning insurance should be retained (Articles 1882–1932 CC) but also the general rules concerning the law of contracts that are found in Book IV of the Civil Code, in which a first section applying to all contracts is then followed by specific provisions concerning typical or nominated contracts.[4]

10. The majority of the rules concerning regulation of insurance companies and intermediaries have been continuously reformed by special laws. In fact, a number of special rules have been approved since 1923 with respect to insurance companies and later to some types of intermediary. There exist also a number of 'sub-legal' rules that have been enacted by the government and by the administrative authorities.

11. In recent years the complexity of the existing rules concerning insurance has reached a dramatic level, especially because of the constant need to implement the European legislation. In addition the Civil Code provisions on insurance contracts

---

3. See A. La Torre, *L'assicurazione nella storia delle idee* (Milan, 1999).
4. See A. Monti & A.M. Musy, in *Introduction to Italian law, supra*, 217ff.

were judged incompatible with the insurance system as they only describe two types of insurance contract, life insurance and non-life insurance.

For all those reasons, in January 2003 a government commission was established in order to revise the complete body of Italian law concerning insurance and to combine it into a Code of Private Insurance – *Codice delle Assicurazioni private* (or CAP).

The final text of the Code of Private Insurance was approved with the *Decreto legislativo* 7 September 2005 Official Gazette No. 209 and published in the Official Gazette No. 239 of 13 October 2005.

The Code of Insurance is composed of nineteen titles (*Titolo I–Titolo* XIX, Articles 1–355) and it now includes all insurance regulations and rules except for those provided in the Civil Code. The Code of Insurance is divided as follows: general provisions (I); access to insurance business (II); exercise of the insurance activity (III); mutual insurances (IV); access to reinsurance business (V); exercise of the reinsurance business (VI); insurance groups (VII); budget of the insurance companies (VIII); insurance intermediaries (IX); motor insurance (X); provisions for special insurance operations (XI); rules concerning insurance contracts and coordination with the Civil Code provisions (XII); transparency and protection of the insured (XIII); provision concerning the supervision of insurance undertakings and insurance intermediaries (XIV); additional supervision rules (XV); rules concerning liquidation and other special procedures applying to insurance companies (XVI); indemnity and liquidation (XVII); sanctions (XVIII); fiscal provisions and final provisions (XIX).

The Code of Insurance came into force on 1 January 2006.

Chapter 4. The European Perspective on Insurance and the Impact of European Legislation on National Law

§1. MOVING FROM ECONOMIC COMMUNITIES TO EUROPEAN UNION

12. The actual shape of Italian insurance law cannot be comprehended without considering the impact of European legislation on national law and a look at the creation of the European single market for insurance. It goes without saying that the history of European insurance law finds its roots in the creation of a new international legal order for Europe, which formally dates back to 1951, when the European Coal and Steel Community was created and followed, a few years later, by the European Economic Community established by the Treaty of 1957.[5]

At that time it was not, in any case, the political and cultural basis that supported and gave strength to the new entities, but instead the search for an economic supranational space and the need for survival in the face of the big forces outside Europe.[6]

Over the past fifty years, the aim and cultural background of the Community have profoundly changed.[7] One of the tangible signs of the progress made on a cultural and substantial level is the will to approve a Constitution for Europe,[8] which makes clear that the transformation and growth is not only in geography and demography, but also pervades the fundamental perception of the European model of integration.[9]

At the same time, the role of the European institutions has changed, as testified by the role of the European Commission, which now plays an essential part in defining the steps to be taken by the European Union and giving shape to the realization of the so-called principle of subsidiarity.[10] As to the role of the different legal

---

5. See V.W.O. Henderson, *The Genesis of the Common Market*, (London, 1962); F. Pocar, *Lezioni di diritto delle Comunità Europee*, (Milan, 1991); D. Weigall &P. Stark, *The Origins and Development of the European Community*, (London, 1992).
6. See generally D. Chalmers, *European Law*, vol. I., *Law and EU Government*, 1998, 5–12.
7. The former name of European Economic Community was changed to the European Community by the Treaty of Maastricht signed on 7 Feb. 1992. The Treaty of Maastricht, modifying some of the competencies of the European (Economic) Community, gave birth to the European Union. This represents a new form of cooperation between the Member States, based on the consolidation of the aims and purposes of the European Community, on the implementation of a common foreign policy, on the protection of the rights and interests of nationals through the introduction of a citizenship of the Union, and on the development of cooperation on justice and home affairs.
8. See for a deeper analysis of the minimal requirement to trace the form of federalism and the role of a constitution, V.K. Lenaerts, 'Constitutionalism and the Many Faces of Federalism', *Am. J. Comp. L.*, 28, 1990, 205.
9. J.H.H. Weiler, *The Constitution of Europe: 'Do the New Clothes have an Emperor?' and other Essays on European Integration*, 1999, 10.
10. Several analyses have tried to focus on the principle of subsidiarity that emerged after the European Union Act. Among others see V.A.G Toth, 'The Principle of Subsidiarity in the Maastricht Treaty', *CML Rev.*, 29, 1992, 1079; R. Cafari Panico, 'Il principio di sussidiarietà e il ravvicinamento delle legislazioni nazionali', *Riv. Dir. Eur.*, 1994, 53–74; G. Strozzi, 'Le principe de subsidiarité dans la perspective de l'intégration européenne: une énigme et beaucoup d'attentes', *Rev. Trim. d. eur.*, 30, 1994, 375; V.K. Lenaerts, 'The Principle of Subsidiarity and the Environment in the European

sources[11] which accompany the creation of the insurance market, legislation is the major one, while the contributions of the European Court have, for a quite long time, been limited and have only recently made a deeper impression.

When looking at the process of integration, it is important to situate this process against the background of the discussion about two different models of 'integration'. The first one, called the neo-realist model, stresses the obstacles to the process of integration due to the need to preserve the individuality of national legal systems.[12] The second model focuses on the intensification of the process of integration and favours an evolution towards a more integrated federal system.[13]

These alternatives are reflected in the different fields of insurance law and have a strong impact on the national legislation. The final result is that, while some aspects of the business are quite satisfactorily regulated at a Community level and express the clear realization of a harmonized system, other areas, such as insurance contract law, are still the victim of a more hazardous process of harmonization.[14]

Union: Keeping the Balance of Federalism', *Fordham Int'l'L. J.*, 1994, 846. The Treaty of the European Community as later revised provides that

'The Community shall act within the limits of the powers conferred upon it by this Treaty and the objectives to it therein. In areas which do not fall within its exclusive competence, the Community shall take action, in accordance with the principle of subsidiarity, only if and insofar as the objectives of the proposed action cannot be achieved by the Member States and can therefore, by reason of the scale or effects of the proposed action, be better achieved by the Community. Any action by the Community shall not go beyond what is necessary to achieve the objectives of this Treaty' (Art. 5, ex Art. 3B). The principle of subsidiarity is intended to regulate the areas in which there is concurrent legislative competence of the Community and the states. The principle of subsidiarity establishes the rule that the Community can act in the areas of concurrent competence in any case in which the proposed action can be better achieved by the Community instead of the states. It is not difficult to understand the expansive force given to the Community. That was clearly recognized in the Protocol to the EC Treaty on the application of the principles of subsidiarity and proportionality: 'Subsidiarity is a dynamic approach concept and should be applied in the light of the objectives set out in the Treaty. It allows Community action within the limits of its powers to be expanded where circumstances so require, and conversely, to be restricted or discontinued where it is no longer justified.'

11. See R. Sacco, *'Introduzione al diritto comparato'* (1990), trans. as *'Legal Formants: A Dynamic Approach to Comparative Law'*, Am. J. Comp. L. 39 1, 1991, 343.
12. L. Antoniolli De Florian, *La struttura istituzionale del nuovo diritto comune europeo. Competizione e circolazione dei modelli giuridici*, 1996, 306.
13. Most recently, analysis of the progress of integration has involved the tools of comparative law and economic analysis of law. See V.J.A. Jolowicz, 'New Perspectives of A Common Law of Europe: Some Practical Aspects and the Case for Applied Comparative Law', in *New perspective for A Common Law of Europe, ed.* M. Cappelletti (Leiden, 1978); U. Mattei, 'Efficiency in Legal Transplant: an Essay in Comparative Law and Economics', *Int.'l Rev.L. Econ.*, 14, 1994, 3; C. Jorges, *Rationalization Process in Contract Law and the Law of Product Safety: Observations on the Impact of European Integration on Private Law*, EUI Working Papers, Law No. 94/5, 1994.
14. From a technical point of view, it is necessary to distinguish quite clearly, in the process of creation of a 'European law', between *unification* of laws, *uniformity of law* and *harmonization*. The process of unification of law is based on a single legislative and authoritarian act and on the fact that the application of the rules is supervised by a sole central authority. That is the case for the European Treaty. In addition, the process of uniformity of laws is related to the approval of regulations and accepts that a common rule is then submitted to the interpretation of national authorities. The harmonization is instead related to the fixing of common aims that the states are then required to implement. The process of harmonization is realized by directives. See Benacchio, G., *Diritto privato della comunità europea*, 2004; R. Sacco, 'I problemi dell'unificazione del diritto in Europa', in *I*

§2. THE EMERGENCE OF A EUROPEAN INSURANCE LAW

13. The creation of a single market for insurance had to face three major types of barrier: the physical, the technical and the fiscal.[15]

While the market itself and the new techniques for selling insurance products, especially the Internet and electronic commerce, are succeeding in destroying the physical barriers, and the fiscal one still remains fixed and stable because of its strict connection with the sovereignty of the single states,[16] the legal-technical barrier has been assaulted by European legislation in different ways.

14. A closer look reveals that the creation of the European market in insurance is based on a process of harmonization of law the aim of which is to realize the Four Freedoms expressed in the original version of the Treaty. According to the recital of the Treaty the internal market should comprise an area without internal frontiers in which the free movement of goods, persons, services and capital is ensured in accordance with the provisions of the Treaty itself.

As insurance is a 'service', the realization of the single market for insurance started with the definition of the programme of the 1960s adopted by the European Commission, and has now reached a quite satisfactory level after the implementation of the third generation directives, as we intend to show, at least with reference to the exercise of insurance business.

15. Nevertheless, it is necessary to remember the many difficulties encountered on the way by the European Commission. The first was that freedom to provide services and consequently exercise insurance business in a single market was strictly connected to and dependent on the existence of free movement of capital.

In addition, the establishment of a single market for insurance had to take into consideration two other aspects: the first one was (and still is) the necessity of a balance between the right of the insurance companies to exercise cross-border operations and the right of consumers to receive (equal) protection from failures of the

---

contratti, 1995; 1, 73–77; S. Ferreri, 'Le fonti normative di produzione non nazionale. Il diritto uniforme', in Rescigno, P. (ed.), *Trattato dir. Priv.*, I, 1982, 153.

15. See McGee, *The Single Market in Insurance: Breaking down the Barriers*, 1998, 6.

16. The regulation of the tax system at a European level in order to get real harmonization is one of the main targets of the European Commission. See European Commission, *The Action Plan 1997* (CSE (97) 1 final, 4 Jun. 1997): 'Dealing with key market distortions. Action one: Remove tax distortion: Tax barriers and distortion to the Single Market have not yet been tackled with sufficient determination. Harmful tax competition increases Member States' difficulties in restructuring their tax systems and delays progress towards a more coherent tax system within the Union. A coordinated approach, as pursued in the Taxation Policy Group, should contribute significantly towards resolving such problems . . . . In this context, consideration could be given to: a code of conduct designed to reduce effectively harmful competition which causes difficulties for every Member State, particularly in the area of corporate taxation; measures to eliminate distortions to the taxation of capital income; measures designed to eliminate withholding taxes on interest and royalty payments between companies, which form part of long-standing efforts to remove tax disincentives to cross-border economic activity (double taxation); measures designed to eliminate significant distortions in the area of indirect tax legislation.' See *again* Communication from the Commission to the European Parliament, the Council, The economic and Social Committee and the Committee of the regions, Strategic objectives 2000–2005 (COM (2000) 154 final).

insurance companies or wrongful conduct. Furthermore, various forms of regulation of insurance business already existed in the European countries at the time of the creation of the European Community both at a legislative and sub-legislative level, so that it was necessary to first create a common basis of administrative authorization for insurance companies and post-authorization supervision of insurers as well as for intermediaries.

16. It should also be borne in mind that the creation of the single market of insurance gives insurers the possibility of carrying out cross-border operations in two different forms, that is to say either in the form of an establishment or merely in the form of providing insurance services without establishing a branch or an agency in the host country.

17. A still closer look demonstrates that freedom of establishment, being the right of a natural or legal person to settle in a Member State and to pursue economic activities there, extends to the right of companies incorporated in one Member State to set up agencies, branches or subsidiaries in any other Member State. Member States may not maintain legislation or enact new legislation which might impede this right except as provided by the Treaty.

Freedom to provide services is the right conferred on a natural or legal person established in one Member State to provide services in another Member State under the same conditions as are imposed by the state on its own nationals. In the field of banking and insurance, this right was at first restricted since such freedom had to be realized in accordance with the freedom of capital movement.[17]

18. The general settings of the Treaty proclaiming the freedom of services then had to be completed by secondary legislation, in accordance with the general principles in the Treaty itself.

The process of integration through harmonization was carried out by directives. As it is commonly known, the specific characteristic of a directive is that it is addressed to the Member States and it is binding upon them as to the result that it is intended to achieve. It is then left to the Member States to decide the ways and methods by which the directive is transformed into national law. This characteristic distinguished directives from regulations, which have general application and are binding in their entirety and directly applicable in all Member States.

19. The law-making process in the creation of the single market for insurance has been carried out on the basis of caution and compromise and it is mainly concentrated around three different pairs of directives which contributed to the realization of the aims expressed by the Treaty and in the General Programme of the European Commission of 1961.

---

17. See for comments A. Arora & X. Favre Bulle, *The Single European Market and the Banking Sector* (1996); D. Swann, *The Single Market and Beyond: a Study of the Wider Implications of the Single European Act*, Routledge, 1993.

The technique of the 'pairs of directives' was used to consolidate the clear separation between life and non-life insurance. The three generations of insurance directives, those for life insurance and the others for non-life insurance, nevertheless maintain a certain specificity in their general settings.

§3. First Directives

20. By way of summary, the first generation insurance directives (Council Directive 73/239 of 24 July 1973 on the coordination of laws, regulations and administrative provisions on the taking up and pursuit of the business of direct insurance other than life insurance and Council Directive 79/267 of 5 March 1979 on the coordination of laws, regulations and administrative provisions on the taking up and pursuit of the business of direct life insurance) laid down a common regulatory structure for insurance companies by fixing some minimal requirements for access to insurance business.

In particular they introduced the requirement of a prior authorization by the national authorities as precondition for the exercise of insurance business. The authorization has to be given for each branch (or class) of business according to a classification made in annexes to the directives.[18]

The first directives also adopted the rule that already existed in most of the Member States, prohibiting the joint exercise of both life and non-life insurance (abolition of the so-called composite insurers), except for companies already authorized to do so at the time of the approval of the Life Directive,[19] and on condition that they maintain separate accounts for non-life and life fund revenues.

In order to obtain authorization the insurance company's assets have to satisfy certain requirements which are now uniform in all the European Member States thanks to the implementation of the directives. The directives require a plan of assets for the insurance company the margin of which has to be calculated under the instructions of the directives (so-called solvency margin).

Access to insurance business is open only to certain types of company.[20] Under the first generation directives, general and special policy terms and anticipated levels of premium income also had to be presented, while as we will see the approval of premium was then abolished, as well as the approval of policy terms. It was then provided that an insurer with a head office in one EC Member State was entitled to establish a branch or agency in another Member State, but subject to specific authorization.

---

18. Since then Europe has consequently had a common division of insurance activity in branches and each insurance contract has to be related to one or the other branch.

19. Italy was among the states to allow the contemporary exercise of life and non-life business. See A. La Torre, *Diritto delle assicurazioni*, vol. I, *La disciplina giuridica dell'attività assicurativa*, 1987; A. Donati, G. Volpe, Putzolu, *Manuale di diritto delle assicurazioni*, fifth edn. 1999.

20. See Art. 8, Third Life Directive.

§4. SECOND DIRECTIVES

21. The Second Generation Directives (Council Directive 88/357 of 22 June 1988 on the coordination of laws, regulations and administrative provisions relating to direct insurance other than life insurance and laying down provisions to facilitate the effective exercise of freedom to provide services and Council Directive 90/619 of 8 November 1990 on the coordination of laws, regulations and administrative provisions relating to direct life insurance laying down provisions to facilitate the effective exercise of freedom to provide services) completed the legal framework for freedom of establishment and partially implemented the freedom of services.

Some further steps were taken in order to ensure the freedom to provide services, especially in two situations: (a) when the insurance covered a large risk;[21] and (b) when it was the decision of the insured person to do business with an insurer established abroad.

Some supplementary rules were added in order to protect consumers who had contracts with companies abroad. The provisions of the Directive on Non-Life Insurance were also extended to compulsory insurance, especially motor liability insurance, previously excluded by the First Non-Life Directive.

It should be noted, however, that these steps were also taken as a result of the principles and assumptions that were adopted in the 1984 insurance cases, that is to say a series of cases decided by the Court of Justice with reference to the implementation of the Co-insurance Directive.[22]

These cases become important for two different reasons: first they offered a clear example of dialogue between the constitutional powers within the European Community (legislative and judicial); secondly, although co-insurance was the object of a separate directive, it is important to realize that the principles expressed by the court on the distinction between freedom to provide services and freedom of establishment also apply to insurance in general.[23]

§5. THIRD DIRECTIVES

22. It was nevertheless only with the appearance of the third generation directives (Council Directive 92/49 of 18 June 1992 on the coordination of laws, regulations and administrative provisions relating to direct insurance other than life

---

21. Large risks are risks of a commercial nature including transport insurance and credit insurance. Property and liability risks are considered large risks when the assured has met the minimum turnover requirement.

22. The insurance cases saw the European Commission against some of the Member States: C 252/83 *Commission v. Denmark*; C 205/84 *Commission v. Germany*; C 206/84 *Commission v. Ireland*; C 220/83 *Commission v. France*. The relevant point was to establish whether domestic rules were not discriminatory or unduly restrictive according to the Co-insurance Directive, which required Member States to lift restrictions on the participation in co-insurance of an insurer established in a Member State with another insurer established in another Member State, so that the foreign insurer did not have to seek authorization in the state in which the leading insurer had its head office. For an overview of the cases and solutions proposed by the court see A. Jannuzzi, *L'assicurazione nel Mercato Unico Europeo*, 1989, 119–130; R. Merkin & A. Rodger, *EC Insurance Law*, 1997, 7–10.

23. See Merkin & Rodger, *EC Insurance Law*, 8.

insurance and Council Directive 92/96 of 10 December 1992 on the coordination of laws, regulations and administrative provisions relating to direct life insurance, as amended by Directive 95/26/EC), also called the single market directives, that the home country control and the single license (or single or European passport) principles were clearly affirmed.

In fact, in the struggle between home state regulation and host state regulation, it was decided – now that the process of harmonization of the preliminary conditions to exercise insurance business had reached a satisfactory level – that an insurance company could act in all the Member States without needing to obtain separate authorization.[24] That means that an insurance company authorized in its original state (home state) does not need a new authorization to exercise cross-border, but only has to make the proper communication to the home country authority which then transmits the information to the host country authority.[25]

In other words, home state authorization will be sufficient to exercise the insurance business abroad both in the form of freedom of establishment and of freedom to provide services.[26]

With the introduction of the single European passport, the major challenge was the reinforcement of the coordination between the authorities responsible for official supervision. Nevertheless, even after the deadline for implementation of the third generation directives had elapsed, the single European passport was not used to its maximum. This was mainly due to the difficulty in distinguishing, in practical terms, between situations that should be qualified as freedom to provide services and as freedom of establishment, and consequently which regime the insurance company had to choose when it intended to distribute its products cross-border.

23. Following the judicial background emerging from the decisions by the European Court of Justice during the past year the European Commission is now trying to set some clear rules applicable to the insurance business; these are incorporated in the Commission Communication on Freedom to Provide Services and the General Good in the Insurance Sector.[27]

Although the official release of the Communication was expected for spring 1997, this deadline was missed and only a preliminary draft circulated for a long time was

---

24. One major point is that Art. 21 deals with the coverage of technical provisions and lists of categories of assets which can be used to cover the technical provision. In fact, Member States are allowed to fix stricter rules. These rules go together with the definition of the financial supervision of an insurance undertaking (see Art. 15).

25. It should be noted that the notification procedure laid down by the third directives only involves an exchange of information between the supervisory authorities and does not affect the validity of insurance policy itself.

26. Even though this is not expressly said in the Treaty or in the directives, an insurance company can carry on activities under the freedom to provide services and at the same time, through some form of establishment in a host country. The insurance company will be required to maintain a separation between the activity under the two forms, so that it can clearly connect the activity to one of the two forms of operation. The same result is clearly expressed in the Commission Interpretative Communication in banking (SEC (97) 1193) and later on in the Commission Interpretative Communication DOC-COM (43/2000).

27. DOC-COM 43/2000.

available to market operators to consider its main statements; these were only later confirmed in the final version of the Communication.

Looking at the Communication, one might think that the Commission just wanted to make the point of the judicial decision. In fact, the Commission is doing something more.

The Commission gives major attention to the relation with an insurance intermediary. In fact, where there are staff dependent on the company, the activity is covered by the provision concerning the right of establishment. On the other hand, when the company acts with independent intermediaries, the distinction between freedom to provide services and freedom of establishment is more difficult to trace, leaving a so-called grey area.

On the basis of the case law of the European Court of Justice, the Commission considers that even a formally independent intermediary can be an establishment of the company in the host state if the following conditions are satisfied: (a) the intermediary is subject to the management and supervision of the insurance undertaking it represents; (b) it is able to commit the insurance undertaking; (c) it has a permanent brief to act on behalf of the company.

In the presence of these conditions, the intermediary will be considered to act as a genuine extension of the insurance company so that the arrangements of the establishment regime are to be observed.

It is consequently a qualitative analysis of the activities made by the intermediary which is relevant to the distinction between the free provision of services and the right of establishment, and not a merely quantitative analysis.[28]

This was clearly in line with the decision *Commission v. Germany*,[29] in which the Court held that:

> an insurance undertaking of another Member State which maintains a permanent presence in the Member State in question comes within the scope of the provisions of the Treaty on the right of establishment, even if that presence does not take the form of a branch or agency, but consists merely of an office managed by the undertaking's own staff or by a person who is independent but authorized to act on a permanent basis for the undertakings, as will be the case with an agency.

In any case, the temporal aspect assumes a fundamental importance because the presence of the intermediary becomes relevant when the selling of insurance products in the host state has a permanent character. It should be noted that the

---

28. According to the Communication an insurance company that decides to transact insurance business under the freedom to provide services must be able to offer certain services in the host state and consequently to use for example a local expert to assess the risk to be covered and to assess damage caused under risks covered, to have a permanent structure for collecting the premiums for insurance policies entered into under the freedom to provide services, to have a permanent structure for receiving notices of claims relating to the policies concluded under the freedom to provide services for transmission to the insurance undertaking for a decision to accept or refuse a claim.
29. C 205/84 [1986] ECR 3755.

permanent nature of the activity has to be determined in the light of its duration, regularity, periodicity and continuity.[30]

Finally, it should be remembered that, with reference to the distinction between freedom to provide services and the right of establishment, the final version of the Communication pays explicit attention to the role of the distribution of insurance products via the Internet, which is undoubtedly an important factor and will have direct influence on the ways in which the freedom to provide services can be exercised. The e-commerce problem was completely ignored in the drafts of the Interpretative Communication. The prevailing opinion was then that 'the initiatives which the Commission has just launched on electronic commerce and the work carried out in the Insurance Committee on the implication of electronic commerce technology of insurance will provide new elements which will have to be taken into account in the interpretation of the Insurance Directives'.[31] The Communication has now taken a position on the problem and decided that cross-border insurance business carried on via electronic commerce must be regarded as insurance business carried on under the freedom to provide services.

The Communication also clarifies that the Member State of establishment of the insurance undertaking with which a policy is concluded in this way is the Member State of establishment of the insurer that effectively carries on the insurance activity (head office or branch) and not the place where the technological means used for providing the service are located (e.g., the place where the Internet server is installed).

24. Another peculiar character of the third directives is the role attributed to the category of the 'general good'. Since the concept of general good has developed in the Court of Justice case law, it is necessary once more to make reference to the decisions of the Court.[32] In simple words, the principle has the effect of extending national powers to impose its rules, as its essential definition is that a host Member State may have recourse to the justification of the general good in order to enforce compliance with its own rules by an insurance undertaking company desiring to carry on business in its territory under the right of establishment or the freedom to provide services.

Such an undertaking company is consequently obliged to comply with a rule of the state which has the effect of limiting its freedom of action if it is considered that the specific national provision satisfies the following criteria: the provision does not come within a field which has previously been harmonized at a Community level; it is a non-discriminatory provision; the provision is justified by imperative reasons relating to the general good (e.g., to consumer protection, fraud prevention, tax system and schemes, protection of workers); the national provision does not duplicate

---

30. C 55/94 *Gebhard* [1995] ECR I-4195: 'A national of a Member State who pursues a professional activity on a stable and continuous basis in another Member State where he holds himself our from an established professional base to, among others, nationals of the State comes under the chapter relating to the right of establishment and into the chapter relating to services.'

31. See CAB XV/207/97.

32. The concept of general good was developed in a series of cases concerning the free movement of goods. A brief account of the rules set out the judicial cases is repeated in McGee, *supra*, 66.

the home country provision; the provision is proportional to the objective pursued.[33]

Once again the Communication illustrates these criteria in practical terms with several examples from the insurance sector.[34] Although the Commission opened consultation among the Member States about what should be considered as a provision relating to the general good, there were no surprising results and the reference to the 'general good' provision remains a hazardous tool in the hands of individual Member States.[35]

Although similar problems were faced by the European Commission with reference to the freedom to provide services for credit institutions, as shown in the Communication on freedom to provide services and the concept of the general good in the second banking directive of 1997,[36] the remaining uncertainties are numerous.

§6. The Lack of European Legislation on Insurance Contract Law

25. The single market directives have created the legal framework implementing the right of establishment and the freedom to provide services. In practical terms

---

33. Consequently, an insurance undertaking doing business through its branches or under the freedom to provide services which is required by the host state to comply with a national provision which has the effect of limiting its freedom of activity may question the application of that provision if it does not satisfy the criteria. It should be noted that the Communication on the bank sector (released on 26 Jun. 1997) set out the six indicated criteria. In particular, as regards the principle of proportionality, the Commission considers that a Member State, when imposing the general good provision, has to make a distinction according to status of the customers, and in particular whether or not the services are supplied to customers who are fully aware of potential risks (especially consumers) and customers who are or may be aware of the potential risks (e.g., frequent investors and large corporate customers).

34. The commission makes a list of provisions which could hardly be protected in the name of national good, for example national provisions requiring absolutely and unconditionally the use of a specific language, national rules imposing standard classes or minimum insurance conditions, national rules requiring the prior notification of policy conditions to the national authorities for supervising insurance policies. In particular, if we limit the analysis to this last point, it is evident that Community law has already fixed a minimum level for which prior communication is required. For an analysis of the problems connected with the application of general good see *C.* Van Schoubreck, 'The Concept of the General Good', in *The Law and Practice of Insurance in the Single European Market,* ed. McGee & Hausel (1994), Market, 1995; G. Parleani, 'Observations sur le projet de la communication de la Commission. Liberté de prestation de services et intérêt général dans le secteur des assurances', RGAT, 1997, No. 4, 1197.

35. It was pointed out that maybe 'in so far as any Member State has identified rules likely to fall into this category, it would probably prefer to protect its tactical position by not admitting openly that these rules required to be justified under the 'general good' exemption. Should the question arise before the Court of Justice, the Member State would no doubt prefer to be in a position still to argue that the rules in question are not incompatible with Arts 52–66, using the 'general good only as a fallback position' (McGee, *supra,* 69).

36. SEC (97) 1193. In fact, the Communication was intended to enable 'credit institutions to operate within a clearer and more precise legal framework, to give fresh momentum to the freedom to provide banking services, thereby increasing the diversity of the banking services offered within the Union and making it easier for those services to be offered across frontiers particularly in the light of the Information Society and the development of electronic trading' (see presentation for the Communication by Financial Services Commissioner Mario Monti).

the insurers are required to apply a high standard of expertise in order to create the so-called Euro products, that is to say insurance products which satisfy the legal requirement of the different legislation on contracts. Such requirements could hinder the easy circulation of products within the EU.

The major obstacle to achieving harmonization in insurance contract law is essentially technical and refers mainly to the existence of a deep connection with general contract law. In other words, insurance contract law remains part of and is consequently governed by the general rules concerning contract law, which in itself is non-harmonized within the European Union.[37] Besides, if a growing amount of European legislation is now enacted, the process of integration is still characterized by fragmentary provisions which should be reorganized, according to some authors, in a systematic form, not least a codification.[38]

According to some authors, the achievement of harmonization of insurance contract law should pass first though the common definition of rules concerning the law of contract. Besides, it should be noted that within the European Union there are some countries in which the insurance contract is governed by a specific and complete body of rules (the French position)[39] while other countries tend to apply to the insurance contract the general rules governing the law of contract.[40]

It should also be noted that the prior control of policy conditions by the national authorities has now disappeared, due to the new regulation introduced by the third directives.

26. The attractiveness of a European insurance contract law was first discussed by jurists a long time ago, and an important step was taken with the Proposal for a directive on insurance contract law.[41]

A simple reading of the premises to the proposal told the reader about the fundamental statements and aims of the text and invited the reader to focus on the areas of insurance contract law which, according to the Commission, were most in need of harmonization in order to ensure adequate protection of the policyholder and the insured.

The central goal was evidently to establish a 'balance between the interests of the insurer on the one hand and the protection of the policyholder and the insured person on the other', the view of the Commission when preparing the draft being in

---

37. H. Kotz & A. Flessner, *European Contract law*, translated by Tony Blair, vol. I, Clarendon Press, 1997; P.D.V. Marsh, *Comparative Contract law: England, France, Germany*, Gower, 1996. See *also* M.J. Bonell, *An international restatement for Contract Law: The UNIDROIT Principles of International Commercial Contracts*, New York, 1994.

38. J. Basedow, 'Un droit commun des contrats pour le marché commun', in RIDC, 1, 1998, 7; in this passage the author expresses the view that the law of contract is the very basis of the formation of a common market and that a codification of European contract law could be realized by a means of a regulation under Art. 100 of the Treaty.

39. As is known, France has a *Code des Assurances*, providing a detailed and systematic embodiment for the insurance contract. See Y. Lambert-Fravre, *Droit des Assurances*, 10th edn. 1997; J. Bigot, (ed.), *Traité des droit des assurances*, vols. I and II, 1996–1997.

40. In Italy, Insurance contracts are taken into consideration in Art. 1882–Art. 1932 of the Civil Code. Nevertheless, this cannot be considered a full comprehensive regulation of insurance contract law, as it only contains general rules, which have to be supplemented with provisions on contract law.

41. (OJ 90/2 dated 28 Jul. 1979).

fact that it seemed necessary to set common rules in favour of the insured party, so as to enable choice between the products of companies established in different states having the same minimum level of protection. The proposed directive was also intended as a measure to improve competition in order to put all EU insurers on the same footing.

According to the European Commission, the author of the proposal, the areas in which harmonization was most necessary were essentially (a) the legal consequences of the declaration on the risk made by the policyholder, both at the time of the conclusion of the contract and during the course of the contract itself; (b) the policyholder's attitude with regard to the measures to be taken and activity to be upheld in case of claim; (c) the effect of the payment (and eventually the failure of payment) on the cover; (d) the duration of the contract; (e) the relation between the insured and the policyholder; (f) information to be given to the policyholder after the conclusion of the contract. Life insurance and many forms of commercial risks (e.g., transport and credit policies) were left out of the Proposal.

Despite the appeal of its laudable aim, the Proposal never made progress and was finally abandoned in 1994, but it remains a sort of guide to the subsequent directives. After the abandonment of the proposal of directive, the harmonization of insurance contract law was left aside for some years on the implicit assumption that sufficient protection of the policyholder had been achieved and that Member States were allowed to apply stricter rules to protect policyholders where these rules were established in their national legislation.

Recently, the attitude to the problem has once again changed: in its last opinion (doc. EESC 1626 of 15 December 2004) the European Economic and Social Committee expressed the need and urgency for harmonization of insurance contract law.

Chapter 5. Government Regulation and Government Agencies: Supervision of Insurance Companies and Other Financial Institutions

§1. ISVAP

I. The Creation of ISVAP

27. The Italian supervisory body for private insurance companies is ISVAP (*Istituto di Vigilanza sulle Assicurazioni Private*). The roles and functions of ISVAP are determined with reference to the Law No. 576, 12 August 1982, and to the Code of Private Insurances, Title I, Chapter 3, Articles 3–10.

ISVAP is endowed with legal status under public law, and it was set up by Law No. 576 of 12 August 1982 for the purpose of supervising insurance companies. Successive insurance regulations have vested ISVAP with additional regulatory and supervisory powers, which have made it fully autonomous in the financial, accounting, organization and management field, while having a specific technical competence and wide operative instruments. Moreover, in 1998 the powers of ISVAP were extended in order to include control over the registers of the agents and insurance brokers.

At present, according to Article 6 of the Code of Private Insurance, ISVAP exercises its supervisory powers over:

(a) insurance and reinsurance undertakings;
(b) financial conglomerates and insurance groups;
(c) every subject or organization operating in the field of the insurance business within the limits of that activity;
(d) insurance intermediaries, insurance experts and all other subjects exercising activity in the insurance business.

ISVAP carries out its duties in keeping with insurance policy lines set by the government.

II. Functions: Supervisory Power

28. According to Article 6 of the Code of Private Insurances, supervision over the insurance market is intended to ensure the prudent and correct exercise of insurance business as well as to guarantee the transparency and fairness of the activity of insurance undertakings and insurance intermediaries. Those activities are to be exercised within the light of the stability, efficiency, competitiveness and correct functioning of the insurance system, and the protection of insured and insurance beneficiaries.

In order to give a concrete meaning to that general assumption, ISVAP exercises financial supervision over insurance undertakings. In particular ISVAP controls whether the technical, financial and accounting management complies with the laws, regulations and administrative provisions in force.

In particular, according to Article 13 of the Code of Private Insurance ISVAP grants undertakings authorization to exercise insurance activity and to extend it to other insurance classes. Moreover it performs all the tasks connected with the granting of authorization, and verifies that all the requirements for the exercise of insurance activity are met.

Of all the prudential supervisory tasks entrusted to ISVAP for the purpose of guaranteeing sound and prudent management of an insurance undertaking, financial supervision assumes particular importance. This supervision consists in monitoring the undertaking's financial position, with particular regard to the existence of a sufficient solvency margin and adequate technical provisions in respect of its entire business, and to the coverage of those provisions by adequate assets.

Since 1998, ISVAP's supervision has extended to insurance intermediaries, for it goes without saying that fairness and transparency in the selling and distribution process play a fundamental role in the development of insurance policy.

III. Control over Insurance Groups and Conglomerates

29. The development of financial activities has led to the creation of more and more numerous and complex groups of insurance undertakings. Hence, taking account of the necessity to supervise relations between companies of the same group in order to assess their impact on the management of each insurance undertaking, ISVAP has been empowered to authorize the acquisition of controlling interests as well as of qualifying holdings in insurance undertakings. Moreover, ISVAP has the power to impose the divestment of stakes held by insurance undertakings if it considers them not to be in line with the business purpose or to be dangerous to the undertaking's soundness. ISVAP is also in charge of the regulation of consolidated accounts of insurance groups. Moreover undertakings must notify ISVAP in advance of certain intra-group financial transactions that they intend to conduct.

Legislative Decrees Nos. 174 and 175 of 1995 implemented the so-called third generation directives in life and non-life insurance and extended the jurisdiction of ISVAP as later confirmed by the Code of Private Insurances. In fact ISVAP must now supervise undertakings having their head office in Italy also as regards the activity they carry on in the EU by way of establishment or of free provision of services, in accordance with the Community principles of home country control and of the mutual recognition of national legislation.

In the performance of its statutory duties ISVAP may request information, data and collaboration from all offices of the public administration; moreover, it promotes all forms of collaboration deemed necessary with the other financial and insurance supervisors of other EU countries.

IV. Investigative Power

30. In the performance of its duties ISVAP may require supervised undertakings to notify data, elements and information. It may conduct on-site inspections and any other type of investigation, as well as summoning the legal representatives, the general manager and the chairman of the board of internal auditors and, where necessary, the representatives of the auditing firm assigned to certify the balance sheet of undertakings.

V. Sanctioning Powers of ISVAP

31. ISVAP can adopt corrective or repressive measures against any undertaking infringing the rules it should observe or behaving in such a way as to jeopardize its soundness.

VI. Regulatory Power

32. Within its statutory powers ISVAP plays a disciplinary role in the insurance market by supervising its compliance with the laws and regulations in force by insurance market participants. ISVAP can issue general and suggest lines of conduct aimed at guaranteeing the necessary link between regulations and the actual reality of insurance practice recommendations and regulations (Article 9, CAP).

VII. Services to Citizens

33. ISVAP is assigned the tasks of collecting complaints made by interested parties against supervised undertakings, facilitating the prompt and correct execution of contracts, asking undertakings for clarifications and making it easier to find a solution to the issues addressed.

It is also worth mentioning that – unlike other European markets – in Italy a so-called insurance 'Ombudsman' does not exist. Nonetheless national legislation has entrusted ISVAP with competence concerning in particular transparency in relations between undertakings and policyholders, as well as information for consumers. ISVAP carries out these functions *vis-à-vis* all undertakings operating on the Italian market, including those having their head office in another EU country and operating in Italy by way of establishment or of free provision of services.

In particular, as for services to citizens, one should mention the fact that ISVAP is assigned the task of collecting complaints made by interested parties against undertaking and insurance intermediaries. The role of ISVAP is better clarified in the Regulation n. 24/2008 – Regolamento n. 24 del 19 maggio 2008- concernente la procedura di presentazione dei reclami all'Isvap di cui all'articolo 7 del decreto legislativo 7 settembre 2005, n. 209.

It should be clear that when dealing with supervisory powers and protection of policyholders, in many aspects the role of ISVAP does not differ towards insured and/or contracting parties where they are consumer or business entities; i.e., as to the regulatory and supervisory powers, the Authority is in charge of assuring transparency in the relation between undertaking and policyholders, whereas this term (policyholder) generally refers both to consumer and non-consumer client. In this role, most of the regulations provided by ISVAP tend to give the market provisions in the direction of assuring the right to information for policyholders and a better transparency in the language and terms of insurance policies.

This clarified, the 'law in action' shows that the role of ISVAP is much more penetrating when dealing for consumer contracts also when considering the mission set by the law: in fact according to Article 3 CAP, ISVAP shall perform the activities necessary to promote an appropriate degree of consumer protection and to develop the knowledge of the insurance market, including statistical and economic surveys and the gathering of input for the formulation of insurance policy lines.

This position has been used, in particular, in order to promote the information on website (see in example www.isvap.it) where specific guides for consumers are present; in other cases, as previously said, the ISVAP prescription – i.e., on information duties in insurance contracts – does not really distinguish between contracts offered to consumer or to businessmen, as the relevant difference is between large risks and other risks (i.e., the case, for example, for pre-contractual duties and delivery of documents duties imposed to insurance intermediaries which apply for all non-large risks).

§2. COVIP

34. COVIP – *Commissione di Vigilanza sui Fondi Pensione* – is an administrative agency, established in 1993 by Legislative Decree No. 124 of 21 April 1993 as a specialist, autonomous public agency for the supervision of pension funds. No 'natural' supervisor for pension funds was in fact available among existing financial supervision authorities (Banca d'Italia, CONSOB, ISVAP).

COVIP supervises all pension funds, except old funds run as book reserve schemes by banks and insurance companies. COVIP supervision instruments are prior licensing, regular and specific reporting, meetings with fund administrators/directors, proposal of fines, dismissal of the board and nomination of a special commissioner, withdrawal of license.

Some regulatory tasks are assigned to the Ministry of Labour and the Ministry of the Treasury.

COVIP has the power to issue regulations on accounting rules, balance sheet schemes, information to pension fund members, selection of investment managers, standard mandate contracts for the management of assets.

COVIP was due to be merged with the market regulator, CONSOB, and the insurance industry regulator, ISVAP, into a single regulatory entity. However, the proposed amalgamation generated a barrage of criticism from a wide variety of sources, including leading trade unions. Instead, closer cooperation of the three regulators will be required, through a formalized system of monthly meetings run by a new umbrella regulator nicknamed 'super-CONSOB'.

§3. BANCA D'ITALIA

35. Banca d'Italia is a fundamental institution of the Italian financial market and it is the most ancient regulatory body. It was created by law in 1893, from a merger between three major private institutions.

The governmental nature of the Banca d'Italia is reflected in many aspects concerning the governance and the interests of the bank. Its responsibilities have kept expanding, including the role of Treasury cashier in the provinces, in 1894, to the overall supervision of banking and financial affairs and the management of monetary policies.

The crisis of the 1930s led to the promulgation of the Banking Law, in 1936, which, in order to grant greater stability to the financial system, also increased the supervisory powers of the Bank of Italy and formally declared it a public law institution. Among its main exclusive functions are the issuance of banknotes, management of monetary and exchange policies, banking and financial supervision – with special regards to the supervision of banks and non-bank intermediaries and their relationship with the credit system – and money and financial market supervision.

Chapter 6. The Italian Association of Insurance Companies: ANIA

36. ANIA is the national association of Italian insurance companies. It has its headquarters in Rome. ANIA is the spokesman for the insurance industry and relates its opinion and standpoints to the government.

ANIA delivers model contracts but does not have any compulsory powers over its associated insurance companies.

Chapter 7. Insurance Law Reviews

37. Sources of information in insurance law are quite varied. Among other things, it is essential to remember two major law reviews concerning insurance law and economics. One is *Diritto e economia dell'assicurazioni*, the other is *Assicurazione*.

A number of papers concerning insurance are also to be found in *Danno e responsabilità civile* (published monthly) and *Responsabilità civile e assicurazione* (quarterly publication).

Selected Bibliography

AA.VV. *Contratti di assicurazione vita, infortuni, Contratti para-assicurativi.* Milan, 1993.

Alpa, G. *Il diritto dei consumatori.* 2nd rev. edn, Bari, 1999.

Benacchio, G. *Diritto privato della comunità europea,* 2004.

Boccia, R. 'Evoluzione e trasformazioni dell'assicurazione "credito" e "cauzioni"'. in *Le assicurazioni del credito e delle cauzioni nel mondo, coll. Quaderno della Rivista Monografica 'Dibattiti rotariani'.* 1974.

Buttaro. *L'interesse nell'assicurazione.* Milan, 1954.

Candian, A.D. *Responsabilità civile e assicurazione.* Milan, 1993.

Candian, A.D. *Forma e assicurazione.* Milan, 1988.

Candian, A., Cerini, D. & Petrone, V. 'Clausole vessatorie e contratti di assicurazione'. in *Le clausole vessatorie nei contratti con i consumatori. Commentario agli articoli 1469bis – 1469-sexies del Codice Civile.* edited by Alpa & Patti. Milan, 1997.

Cannata, A. & Gambaro, A. *Lineamenti di Storia della giurisprudenza europea.* Turin, 1984.

Capotosti, R.A. *La riassicurazione, Il diritto delle assicurazioni.* 2, Turin, 1991.

Cerini, D. *Assicurazione e garanzia del credito. Prospettive di comparazione.* Milan: Giuffré, 2003.

Cerini, D. *Prodotti e servizi assicurativi. Distribuzione e intermediazione.* Milan: Giuffré, 2003.

Criscuoli, G. & Pugsley, D. *Italian Law of Contract.* Naples, 1991.

De Nova, G. *Il tipo contrattuale.* Padua, 1974.

De Strobel, D. *L'assicurazione della responsabilità civile.*

De Zuliani, G. *Le assicurazioni del credito e delle cauzioni,* Ed. Assicurazioni Generali, 1973.

Donati, A. *Trattato delle assicurazioni private,* 3 vols, Milan, 1952–55.

Donati-Volpe Putzolu. *Manuale delle assicurazioni private,* Milan, 2003.

Ferrarini, S. *Le assicurazioni marittime.* 3rd edn, Milan, 1991.

Fragali, M. voce *Assicurazione del credito,* in *EGI.*

Gambaro, A. & Sacco, R. *Sistemi Giuridici Comparati,* 2nd edn, Turin, 2003.

Gambino, A. *Contratto di assicurazione. Profili generali, Enciclopedia Giuridica,* III.

Henderson, V.W.O. *The Genesis of the Common Market.* London, 1962.

La Torre, A. (ed.). *Le assicurazioni. L'assicurazione nei codici. Le assicurazioni obbligatorie.* Milan, 2000.

Selected Bibliography

La Torre, A. *L'assicurazione nella storia delle idee*. Milan, 1999.

Lena, J.S. & Mattei, U. (eds). *Introduction to Italian Law*. Kluwer, 2002.

Monti, A. *Buona fede e assicurazione*. Milan: Giuffré, 2000.

Navarrini, U. *Trattato elementare di diritto commerciale*. vol. I, 1932-X, 3rd edn, 344.

Partesotti, G. & Ricolfi, M. (eds). *La nuova disciplina dell'impresa di assicurazione sulla vita in attuazione della terza direttiva*. 2000.

Pocar, F. *Lezioni di diritto delle Comunità Europee*, Milan, 1991.

Prosperetti, E.A. & Apicella. *La riassicurazione*, Milan, 1994.

Sacco, R. & De Nova, G. 'Il contratto'. in *Trattato di Diritto Civile*, ed. Rodolfo Sacco, Turin, 1993.

Scalfi, G. *I contratti di assicurazione. L'assicurazione danni*, Turin, 1991.

Scalfi, G. *Manuale delle assicurazioni private*, EGEA: Milan, 1994.

Vivante, C. *Il codice di commercio commentato. Il contratto di assicurazione, di pegno, di deposito nei magazzini generali*. Turin, 1936.

Vivante, C. 'La prescrizione in materia di assicurazioni'. in *Trattato di diritto commerciale*. Milan, 1935.

Volpe Putzolu, G. 'L'assicurazione'. in *Trattato di diritto privato* (ed. Rescigno), 13, Turin, 1985.

Volpe Putzolu, G. *Le assicurazioni. Produzione e distribuzione*. Il Mulino: Bologna, 1992.

Watkin, T.G. *The Italian Legal Tradition*. Ashgate, 1997.

Weigall, D. & Stark, P. *The Origins and Development of the European Community*. London, 1992.

Part I. The Insurance Company

Chapter 1. General Rules on Insurance Company Regulation

§1. ITALIAN INSURANCE COMPANIES

I. Legal Sources of Insurance Company Regulation

38. The essential role of insurance business in our society and the damage that the insolvency of insurance companies can cause to insured persons, beneficiaries and third parties have led to the installation of a close control over access to and the exercise of insurance business.

Italian legislation has consequently regulated access to business since the beginning of the nineteenth century. In 1912 the creation of a public insurance company called INA (*Istituto Nazionale delle Assicurazioni* – National Institute for Life Insurance) was intended as a first step to regulating the market. The intention of the law was to introduce INA's monopoly rights in the offer of life insurance. This monopoly was in fact never realized and it was finally and formally abolished with the Royal Decree 29 April 1923 No. 966. The approval of the Royal Decree 966/1923 was a fundamental step in the regulatory system, as it was the first law to introduce a systematic discipline for the exercise of the insurance business in Italy.

The Royal Decree No. 966/1923 was then fully substituted by the Decree of the President of the Republic (DPR) 13 February 1959 No. 449 (also named *Testo Unico sulle Assicurazioni*), which remained the basic text until the reception of the European directives concerning the carrying out of the insurance activity. Royal Decree No. 966/1923 and the DPR 449/1959 together contained a very prudent regulation by limiting access to the business and by imposing a system of prior authorization, which was at that time to be given by the Ministry of Industry and Commerce.

National legislation also imposed on insurance companies the constitution of minimum capital and technical provisions.

39. The coming of European legislation partially modified the existing law. Legislative Decrees Nos. 174 and 175 of 17 March 1995, now included in the Code of Private Insurances, implemented the third generation of insurance directives of 1992 and replaced the existing law even though the major requirements for authorization and exercise remained unaltered in their substance.[42]

At the same time, all powers of control over insurance companies were transferred to ISVAP, instead of the Ministry of Industry, with a view to strengthening the power of the authority and to concentrating the power of supervision in a single body.

II. Access to Business

40. According to Article 13 *of CAP* access to and the exercise of the insurance business are allowed to companies established under the forms of government-controlled institutions, joint-stock companies (*società per azioni*, regulated by Articles 2325 et seq. CC), cooperative societies with limited liability (*società cooperative a responsabilità limitata* – Article 2511 CC) and mutual companies (*mutue assicuratrici* – Article 1884 CC). Public insurers and social insurance institutions are consequently excluded from the general discipline and follow other ad hoc rules.[43]

41. Although quite common in the past, cooperative societies with limited liability are actually seldom used. Much more widespread are mutual insurance companies. They are regulated by the same rules of the Civil Code concerning stock companies within the limit compatible with a mutual agreement nature (Article 1884 CC). Currently, the activity of mutual companies is based on premium computation. The system of contributing pro quota in mutual insurance companies is currently prohibited.

42. A prerequisite for the beginning of the carrying out of the insurance activity is public authorization, which is given by ISVAP and then published in the Official Journal.

The authorization is given provided the scope of the insurance company is limited to the exercise of insurance activity and to those businesses connected with insurance (Articles 11 and 14 Codice delle Assicurazioni Private).[44]

The goal of this rule, derived from the European legislation, is to preserve the insurance fund and to prevent its use to finance other more speculative or uncontrolled activities.

The specific interpretation of the limits to the insurance companies' business has given rise to many doubts, as there is no clear guidance in law on when exactly a business is connected with insurance.

---

42. See for a complete comment on Legislative Decree No. 175/1995 G. Partesotti & M. Ricolfi, (eds.), *La nuova disciplina dell'impresa di assicurazione sulla vita in attuazione della terza direttiva*, 2000.

43. See G. Partesotti, 'Commento alla legge 10 giugno 1978 No. 195 sub Arts 1–5', in NLCC, 1979, 1093, and G. Bonfante, in Partesotti-Ricolfi, *supra*, 73ff.

44. G.Volpe Putzolu, 'L'assicurazione', in *Trattato di dir.priv.* (ed. Rescigno) (Turin, 1985), 13.

43. The authorization to exercise is given for a single branch of activity. The law prohibits a new applicant from being authorized both in life and non-life insurance, in respect of the principle of the 'non-cumulating'. This rule represents a European novelty as it is intended to prevent the fund and assets of life insurance being used for other purposes. For this reason, the limit of cumulating life and non-life businesses does not apply to insurance companies authorized prior to 15 March 1979, when the first European directive was notified. The so-called multi-branch companies authorized prior to March 1979 represent the large majority of the Italian market. They are obliged to keep separate management and accounting for life and non-life activities.

44. In order to obtain authorization, the insurance undertaking created under a proper form of law has to prove the existence of the minimum capital requirements with reference to the branches for which the authorization is required.

The capital base necessary to obtain authorization is actually EUR 5 million for life insurance, for liability insurance, for credit insurance and guarantee businesses; it is EUR 2.5 million for accident, disease, vehicle and fire insurance; it is EUR 1.5 million for all other branches.

45. The company has to deposit all the documents proving the necessary information – such as the act of constitution of the company, the list of persons in charge of the representation and administration, the list of shareholders with relevant participation in the company (see for more details Articles 68 et seq. of CAP) – to ISVAP.

The insurer must submit a scheme of operations setting out its plan of activity as well as its business and financial projections. The content of the activity plan is set by Article 14(d) CAP and it is intended to prove the compatibility between the projections and the company structure and assets. The same procedure is applied if the company requires an extension of its authorization to operate in other branches, except in respect of the non-cumulating rule between the exercise of life and non-life insurance mentioned above.

46. Following European requirements, Italian law and further decrees establish specific requisites for persons entitled to administer insurance companies. Ministry Decree No. 186 of 24 April 1997 has specifically determined the requisites of honour and professional competence for the heads of the insurance companies in order to ensure that the controllers of the insurance company are fit and proper persons.

47. The provision of authorization by ISVAP is considered obligatory as far as all the requisites set by law are present. That is because, after the third European directives, the power of the state (and of its administrative agencies) to limit a new authorization has been cancelled.

48. The undertaking's authorization to exercise the insurance business automatically expires if the company does not begin the activity within one year from the publishing of the authorization in the Italian Official Journal.

49. After the authorization has been obtained, control over the insurance company is continued by ISVAP, which maintains the supervision and the power to sanction the insurance companies through their life time. For example, the solvency control of insurance companies is constantly executed by ISVAP, to which all companies must submit their annual accounts.

50. A number of further supervisory activities are undertaken by ISVAP during the exercise of the insurance business. In particular, ISVAP can prohibit the acquisition of new contracts if the insurance company violates the rules of technical reserves and does not comply in due time with the prescriptions required by ISVAP.

In case of serious failure and non-compliance with the rules concerning the carrying out of the insurance activity (i.e., if the insurance company does not respect the solvency margin and does not remedy it within the required time), ISVAP can first prohibit the subscription of new contracts and ultimately revoke the authorization to carry on insurance business.

III. Termination of Insurance Activity and Liquidation

51. Insurance companies can terminate their activity following the opening of a voluntary liquidation; this possibility is regulated by the rules provided for stock companies (Articles 2448–9 CC) implemented by those specified for insurance and provided by Articles 228 et seq. CAP, in order to protect the rights of those insured and creditor parties.

In addition to ordinary causes of liquidation, an insurance company is liquidated in case of the revocation of its authorization, the expiry of time of its authorization and compulsory administrative liquidation (*liquidazione coatta amministrativa*).

52. The voluntary liquidation procedure is supervised by ISVAP, which has to approve the nomination of the liquidators appointed by the company.

53. Compulsory administrative liquidation is a cause of termination of activity and it represents the sole collective procedure for insolvency applicable to insurance companies. When such a procedure is opened, special rules are provided in order to protect the rights of creditors and insured persons. The procedure is opened by a decree of the Ministry of Industry under proposal of ISVAP and it is supervised by ISVAP itself.

Insurance contracts at the date of liquidation continue for sixty days after the decree of liquidation, even though the insured have the right to terminate the contract. The liquidator can transfer existing contracts.

IV. Acquisition of Shares

54. The acquisition of shares in and by insurance companies is regulated by Articles from 68 to 75 of the *Codice delle Assicurazioni Private.*

A system of prior notification is required for the acquisition of shares by insurance companies in other companies if the acquisition passes the limit of 5%.

Prior approval of ISVAP is required for the acquisition of controlling shares. Approval will be denied if the activity of the target company is not insurance or insurance related. Similarly, the acquisition of more than 5% of shares of an insurance company must be notified to ISVAP within thirty days. If the acquisition, alone or together with the share already possessed, gives control over the insurance company, prior approval by ISVAP is required.

V. Internal Control: Auditing and Appointed Actuary

55. All insurance companies must have an internal auditing system. The characteristics and role of the internal audit were set by an ISVAP bulletin dated 3 March 1999 No. 366/D.

The social and economic importance of life and motor liability insurance and the complexity of the setting of premiums and rates as well as of technical reserves induced the legislator to require that each insurance company operating in life branches or in motor liability insurance has an appointed actuary.

According to Articles 31 and 34 of CAP, the actuary in charge may be an employee of the company or an outside professional registered in the professional list of actuaries with a certified experience in life or motor liability insurance activity.

The actuary has the task to verify the technical criteria, the statistical methods and the cash flow of the company and to report in the prescribed form to ISVAP.

VI. Foreign Operations by Italian Insurance Companies

56. According to the principle of home country control, ISVAP is given the power to regulate and supervise the EC-wide activity of Italian insurers. ISVAP will consequently supervise the foreign activity of Italian companies in cooperation with host state control authority. Insurance companies must notify to ISVAP a separate account for their foreign activities and distinguish them under the freedom to provide services and the freedom of establishment (Articles 1–18 CAP).

§2. ACTIVITY OF FOREIGN COMPANIES IN ITALY

57. After the implementation of the third generation directives and the Legislative Decrees Nos. 174 and 175 of 1995, a large number of foreign companies have started to carry out their activity in Italy, both by increasing the number of insurers operating under the right of establishment and also by activities under the freedom to provide services, especially in life insurance branches. Access to the Italian market has been with the cooperation of ISVAP and foreign control authorities, as provided by the system of the home country control.

58. Looking more closely at the existing situation, EU companies can operate in Italy either under the freedom to provide services or under the freedom of establishment (Articles 23–28 of CAP).

Pursuant to the freedom of establishment, the supervisory authority of the home country of the insurance company must provide ISVAP with information concerning the characteristics of the company and its plan of activity in Italy. In particular, the documentation produced by the company must include all the elements which are necessary to prove the correct access to the business in its state of origin. In particular: a certificate stating that the insurance company is authorized to do insurance in its home state; a certificate stating that the company possesses the minimum margin of solvency; a plan of the company's activities specifying which risks and obligations the company intends to undertake as well as the organization of the branch; a documentation attesting the appointment of a legal representative in Italy; further elements required specifically for the exercise of activities in non-life branches.

59. The documentation is transmitted by the foreign supervisory authority to ISVAP.

Within sixty days, ISVAP must provide the conditions to be met by the applicant. The company can begin operations after the approval of ISVAP has been issued. Should ISVAP not respond within sixty days, the insurance company is entitled to operate in Italy.

60. If the foreign company wants to act under the freedom to provide services, a similar procedure is provided. In addition to the information mentioned above, the documentation must include the name of the tax representative in Italy.

The foreign insurance company can apply the legislation of the country of origin, provided that certain principles of general interest are not violated. Further rules are set in order to ensure transparency and the correctness of the company's conduct and to protect clients' interests.

Chapter 2. Consumer Protection in Insurance

§1. The Need for Special Protection for Consumers

61. In Italy as well as in other modern countries the need for a special protection of consumers in business-to-consumer relations arose in the final decades of the twentieth century. Because of the imbalance of the contractual power of the professional *vis-à-vis* the consumer, a number of regulations were adopted in order to protect the consumer and the user of professional services here included insured parties.[45]

More specific details will be offered in the different parts of the work. For the moment, in order to give a spectrum of the different actions in the consumer protection laws relating to insurance, some preliminary remarks can be made. In this direction, one should remember that the Code of Private Insurances, and the Civil Code in the articles on contract and on insurance contract, provide no special protection for consumers as such (even if in most cases private insureds are also consumers). Anyway, the weaker party of an insurance relationship enjoy some protection in different ways, as it will be specified for each issue.

In few, specific cases, the Code of Consume provides rules and tools useful also in insurance contracts. The main tool, establishing a very special protection for consumers, is the regulation of unfair contract terms, which nevertheless has not been applied to insurance contracts in meaningful ways.[46]

62. The above-mentioned Article 3 of the Code of Private Insurances[47] states that the control on insurance activities aims, among other goals, at policyholders protection and at information and protection of consumers. As specified by Article 5, the control on insurance activities and all useful acts in order to obtain consumers protection are exercised by the ISVAP (Istituto per la Vigilanza sulle Assicurazioni Private e di interesse collettivo), the Italian Insurance Authority. The ISVAP is entitled to enact regulations (Regolamenti) and to use a long range of powers (for instance, see *infra*, about premium).

63. The inspiration of the Code of Private Insurances and of the ISVAP's powers in light of consumer protection policy are very important in order to understand many rules introduced both in the Civil Code and in the c.a.p. In fact, as we will explain, many of these rules have to be applied to every insured party and not only to consumers. Nevertheless, many of them are typical consumer protection tools (for instance, cooling off periods, ius poenitendi, information duties, etc.), even if they apply to the parties of an insurance contract despite of the qualification of the weaker one as consumer. For that reason, in the following answers all tools will be

---

45. The first, very important, applications of the unfair contract terms directive in insurance contracts were the actions conducted by the associations of consumer in order to ban some clauses from the general conditions of insurance. They were pre-emptive actions, for which, please, refer to the present report, para. III.3.
46. See Ch. 5 above.
47. Provvedimento AGCM, respectively, nr. 18586, in *Bollettino AGCM* nr. 26 of 14 Aug. 2008, and nr. 20007, in *Bollettino AGCM* nr. 26 of 25 Jun. 2009.

highlighted, even if distinguishing between areas in which consumers enjoy special protection and areas in which policyholders or insured parties enjoy protection by means of rules inspired by consumer protection policy.

64. In the area of information duties (and rights), consumer protection is given above all by the Code of Consume. The Code of Consume provides general rules, which must be applied in all activities, and contracts, involving a consumer. The most important provisions are:

- Article 2, paragraph 2, which recognizes to consumers and users some fundamental rights, such as the right to adequate information and to fair advertising (sub c)), the right to the exercise of commercial practices with good faith, fairness, and loyalty (sub c-bis)), and the right to fairness, transparency and equity in contractual relationships (sub e)).
- Article 5, paragraph 3, providing that all information to consumer have to be adequate to the kind of communication used and expressed in understandable way, also keeping into consideration the way to conclude the contract and the specific features of the field, in order to obtain the awareness of the consumer.
- Articles 20 et seq. forbidding unfair commercial practices, among which unfair or misleading advertising (for instance, some cases decided by the Autorità Garante per la Concorrenza ed il Mercato, the Italian Antitrust Authority, concerned advertising of life insurance products, and advertising of benefits promised to consumers buying motor liability insurance[48]).
- Articles 67*bis* et seq. fixing specific rules about information to be given to consumers, in cases of distance selling of financial services.

Apart from the Code of Consume, under the Italian Civil Code, no special rules are provided in order to ensure consumers with proper information before and after the conclusion of the contract of insurance.

65. On the contrary, under insurance contract law, the insured underwrites a proposal (which the insurer considers for acceptance), and therefore is supposed to have knowledge of the terms and conditions of the policy. This is the traditional assumption underlying the qualification of the contract of insurance as a contract of utmost good faith in most legal systems.[49] Nevertheless, the matter of information asymmetries in insurance contracts has been recently read with more attention to the

---

48. Please, see: V. SALANDRA, *Assicurazione*, in *Commentario al Codice Civile*, a cura di A. SCIA-LOJA e G. BRANCA, sub Arts 1861-1932, Capo XX, Bologna-Roma, 1966, III edn. 172-441; and G. Fanelli, *Le assicurazioni*, in *Trattato di diritto civile e commerciale*, diretto da A. CICU e F. MESSINEO, vol. XXXVI, t. 1, Milano, Giuffrè, 1973; A. Gambino, *La neutralizzazione dei rischi nella struttura e nella funzione giuridica unitaria del contratto di assicurazione*, in *Riv. dir. comm.*, 1985, II, 209-221; A. Antonucci, *L'assicurazione fra impresa e contratto*, Bari, 2000; C. Russo, *Trasparenza ed informazione nel contratto di assicurazione*, Padova, 2001; V. De Lorenzi, *Contratto di assicurazione. Disciplina giuridica e analisi economica*, Padova, 2008.
49. A.D.Candian, *Contratto di assicurazione e clausole vessatorie*, in *Le clausole vessatorie nei contratti con i consumatori*, a cura di G. ALPA e S. PATTI, Milano, 1997, t. II, 955; A. Monti, *Buona fede e assicurazione*, Milano, 2002; M. Gagliardi, *Il contratto di assicurazione. Spunti di atipicità ed evoluzione del tipo*, Torino, Giappichelli, 2009.

real knowledge and to the contractual power of the applicant.[50] In fact, and among many other provisions, in order to keep in balance the positions of the parties, both the Civil Code and the Code of Private Insurances contain some rules requiring some kind of information which the insured party ought to receive before or after the conclusion of the contract. As said before, many of these rules are certainly inspired by a consumer protection policy, but they apply to applicants and insureds as such, thus not only to consumers. However, Article 120, paragraph 5, c.a.p. states that intermediaries' duties of information do not apply to policies covering large risks and to contracts of reinsurance, thus excluding from general protection (only) professionals and undertakers.

66. Information concerned are:

(a) pre-contractual information about the insurer and/or about intermediaries involved;[51]
(b) pre-contractual advise about the kind of policy needed, balanced with reference to specific personal features of the insured person;[52]
(c) pre-contractual information related to the main features of the policy (including both explanation from the intermediary and the provision of copy of all the conditions of insurance);[53]
(d) contractual information embodied in the contract, i.e.: the contract and all documents ought to be clear, understandable and complete; moreover, in the contract, terms and conditions imposing on the insured specific duties or warranties must be highlighted and specifically underwritten;[54]
(e) post-contractual (during contract execution) information, particularly in motor liability insurance, concerning the procedure and the evaluations of the insurer in order to pay the insured indemnity to the policyholder;[55]
(f) pre-contractual information, in life insurance, about the financial value of the contract, the costs and risks of the contract and, more particularly, in financial insurance products (such as index-linked policies), for which information provided must include (during all the time of contract validity) also the results of managed investments;[56]
(g) specific rules are provided for pre-contractual information in distance selling (Article 121 of Code of Private Insurances);

---

50. Articles 185 and 120 of the Code of Private Insurances, as specified in the Regolamento Isvap nr. 5/2006. In particular, Art. 120, para. 2, c.a.p.: insurance intermediaries ought to declare whether they have any duty to offer products of one or more insurers or if they give independent advise.
51. Article 120, paras 3 and 4, of the Code of Private Insurances, as specified in the Regolamento ISVAP nr. 5/2006.
52. Article 120, paras 3 and 4, of the Code of Private Insurances, as specified in the Regolamento ISVAP nr. 5/2006 and Art. 185 c.a.p. on the so-called "nota informativa" (information brief document).
53. Article 166 of the Code of Private Insurances, and Arts 1341 and 1342 of the Civil Code.
54. Articles 148 and 149 of the Code of Private Insurances, and d.p.r. 18 luglio 2006, n. 254, particularly Art. 9.
55. Article 1925 of the Civil Code and Art. 185, para. 4, of the Code of Private Insurances.
56. Article 177, para. 2, of the Code of Private Insurances.

(h) pre-contractual information about the right to withdrawal (ius poenitendi) in life insurance contracts.[57]

67. All information duties just listed apply to every insurance contracts, even if their inspiration could be found also in consumer protection policy. As said before (in the present report, paragraph IV), the interaction among different codes is not clear. In particular, in insurance contracts the coordination of the rules contained in the c.a.p. with the ones expressed by the Code of Consume and by the Civil Code is both difficult and of fundamental importance.

In this perspective, it is possible to read the above-mentioned information duties together with the provisions of Articles 2 and 3 of the Code of Consume. This way, the distinction between consumers and non-consumer insureds could be drawn in the sense of a stricter interpretation of the duties when a consumer is involved. However, the real existence and scope of such a distinction depends on the interpretation given to the issue of interaction and coordination among codes.[58]

68. A particular form of consumer protection consists in transparency and comparability of premiums and tariffs, with specific applications in the field of motor liability insurance. The Code of Private Insurances (Articles 131 and 133) requires insurers of motor liability insurance, as far as policies constructed on a experience-rate basis (bonus-malus policies) are concerned, to give notice on their websites and in the premises of their intermediaries (agents) of the premiums applied for each of the categories of insureds.

69. Moreover, the Italian Insurance Supervisory Agency (ISVAP), even if it is not allowed by EC law to require insurers a systematic and preventive communication of the tariffs applied, is allowed to investigate on the rationales used by insurers in calculating premiums and in fixing the tariffs. The compatibility of this power with EC law, together with the utility of the tool in order to protect consumers, has been stated and recognized recently by the European Court of Justice in the decision of 28 April 2009, case *European Commission v. Italy*.

70. Another important reference to be made is to the discipline on Unfair Commercial Practices. Law references are to Articles 20 et seq. of the Code of Consume, implementing the European Directive nr. 2005/29/CE,[59] Besides the unfair or misleading advertising, the Autorità Garante per la Concorrenza ed il Mercato (the Italian Antitrust Authority), AGCM, has decided some insurance cases in which the

---

57. The matter of interaction and of systematic coordination among codes is studied in the same light of the relationship between Civil Code and special legislation. See F.D. Busnelli, *Il diritto civile tra codice e legislazione speciale*, Napoli, 1984 and, with specific attention to insurance contracts, F.D. Busnelli, *Prefazione* a *Le assicurazioni private*, a cura di G. ALPA, Torino, 2006, I.

58. European Directive 2005/29/CE of the European Parliament and of the Council of 11 May 2005 concerning unfair business-to-consumer commercial practices in the internal market "Unfair Commercial Practices Directive", in OJEU L 149 of 11 Jun. 2005, 22–39.

59. Provvedimenti AGCM nr. 19655, in *Bollettino AGCM* nr. 12 of 14 Apr. 2009, and nr. 20158, in *Bollettino AGCM* nr. 30 of 29 Jul. 2009.

insurers (or their intermediaries) acted without due diligence in managing the termination of the contract by the insured parties.[2, 3]

71. Even though it is not in the scope of this text to deal extensively with the policy of consumer protection, a few steps in the long process that led to the creation of a substantial policy on consumer law must be explained. An important step in putting in place the legal basis for a systematic approach to consumer law was the adoption of the Law 30 July 1998 No. 281. The law introduced a special set of rules concerning the organization of consumers' associations and actions in law.

72. With reference to contract law and its impact on insurance, a further crucial time for Italian consumer protection legislation was undoubtedly the implementation of Directive 93/13/EC with the consequent addition of Articles 1469*bis*–1469*septies* of Book IV of the Civil Code. Those articles have now been replaced by the new rules in the Code of Consumer Law: in fact, legislative Decree 6 September 2005 No. 206 titled *Riassetto delle disposizioni vigenti in materia di tutela dei consumatori – Codice del consumo*[60] (Code of Consumer Law) was approved. The cultural and legal impact of the *Codice del Consumo* is strong: once in force, not only will the *Codice del Consumo* unite in a single text the majority of the rules concerning consumer law, but it will also represent a true revolution in the legislative approach to consumer policies.

§2. THE DEFINITION OF CONSUMER IN LAW NO. 281 OF 30 JULY 1998 AND THE DEFINITION IN THE CODICE DEL CONSUMO

73. The Law 281/1998 defined the 'consumer' of products or services as a person who acts for a scope other than that of his/her profession (Article 2). The definition has been reproduced in the *Codice del Consumo* (Article 3(1)).[61] The criteria for the qualification of 'consumer' consequently derive from a combination of a subjective element (a physical person) and an objective element (the scope of the activity or the contract not related to the profession).

This definition must be applied every time and in future texts where the legislator generally refers to consumers (*consumatore*) or to service users (*utenti*).

It is important to note that no extensive interpretation is given to the notion of 'consumer' by the Italian courts. Similarly, the courts have consistently refused to apply the protection provided for consumers in situations where a possible abuse of economic or contractual power between professionals exists.

The Law No. 281/1998 created the *Consiglio Nazionale dei Consumatori e degli Utenti* (CNCU – National Council for Consumers and Service Users), which operates within the Ministry of Industry, Commerce and Craftsmen (new rule Article 136 *Codice del Consumo*).

---

60. See for a complete analysis G. ALPA, *Il diritto dei consumatori*, 2nd revised edn. Bari, 1999, in particular the introduction, at 3–20.
61. In Official Gazette No. 235 of 8 Oct. 2005 – Ordinary Supplement No. 162. For a first comment see M. Dona, *Il codice del consumo. Regole e significati, Introduzione*, Turin, 2005, 1–20.

Representatives of consumers' associations and of the regions and autonomous provinces compose the CNCU. The Prime Minister on the proposal of the Minister of Industry nominates the head official.

74. The legislative authorities have given the CNCU a number of powers and duties in the direction of improving consumer protection and coordinating the activity of consumers' associations with market functioning. Its essential task is to contribute to the improvement and reinforcement of the position of consumers and service users in the market. In fact, the safeguard of the role of the consumer constitutes one of the essential preconditions for ensuring that the market functions in a proper and transparent way.

75. The law vests the CNCU with several duties. Among its institutional tasks stands the duty to express its opinion on laws in preparation if those laws affect or relate to consumers, to formulate proposals concerning consumer protection in general, even with reference to European programmes and politics, to promote studies on problems concerning consumer protection and control over the security of products and services, to elaborate programmes for the information of consumers, to promote procedures for access to justice by consumers and to coordinate national, regional and international activities concerning the protection of consumers (Article 4 of Law 281/1998).

The Council's programme of activities takes place within this perspective and the strategic objectives arising from it. Since its creation Council has been particularly looking at the priorities identified by the European Commission. As a whole those programmes intend to achieve the aim of improving and promoting the interests of consumers and service users, the priorities relate to various economic and social sectors (such as safety of food and food products, services in the public interest, environmental issues, access to justice, the Internet and new technology) including financial services and insurance in particular.

76. Answering a need expressed by different parties, Law No. 281/1998 has established a public register of associations of consumers that correspond to the criteria of representativeness set by the law itself. In fact, before the creation of that register the main risk consisted in a distortion of the representative role of consumers' rights.

Law No. 281/1998 also lists the fundamental rights of consumers and service users and lists the powers of registered consumers' associations (the list is now compiled by the Ministry of Production). In particular, they have a power of action to protect the common interest, both via the office of conciliation and the promotion of alternative dispute resolution systems and also with a possible recourse to the courts.

Another important result of the law was the establishment of the National Council of Consumers and Service Users (CNCU), extending to the publishing activities of the associations inscribed in the register, the facilities and financial contributions provided for by the Law of 5 August 1981, No. 416.[62]

77. An important step in the activity of the Council concerning in the field of financial services was the Insurers–Consumers Associations Agreement (often referred to as the Protocol) signed on 25 October 2000.

The Protocol – which was signed at the end of a round table meeting of the Ministry of Industry, ISVAP, ANIA and CNCU consumers – deals with projects, proposals and measures aimed at containment of the cost of policies for automobile insurance, and at the improvement of services and of competition within the sector.

The activity of the cooperation between the two associations continues with reference to the reform of the rules on personal injuries, which has a close impact on insurance premiums.

§3. The Protection of Consumers through the Sanctions on Unfair Contract Terms

78. The protection of consumers against unfair contract terms represents a fundamental step in the direction of promoting a higher standard of fairness in business to consumers relations. In the Italian legal system such protection is built on two different sets of rules.

The first one coincides with the 'general rules' for standard form contracts in all types of contract notwithstanding the status of contracting consumers: this regulation is to be found in Article 1341 CC, first and second comma; consumers may benefit from additional protection deriving from Articles 33–38 of *Codice del Consumo*.

79. Article 1341 CC provides a basic protection of all contracting parties (both consumers and professionals) who adhere to a standardized contract.

In its first comma, the article establishes the principle of knowledge (*principio di conoscibilità*) according to which standard conditions prepared by one of the parties are binding on the other party if, at the time of formation the contract, the latter knew of them or should have known of them by using ordinary diligence.

Article 1341, CC, comma II, strengthens this rule by stating that, in any case, some conditions and terms are ineffective unless specifically approved in writing if they provide – in favour of the person who has prepared them – limitations of liability, the power of withdrawing from the contract, the suspending of the performance and other onerous clauses.

It is clear that the article provides 'formal' protection to all contracting parties under the requirement of a double signature as a proof of specific approval of these clauses.

There is no doubt that, at the time of approval of the Civil Code (1942), this rule represented a truly innovative discipline. The passing of the years and the need for

---

62. 'Consumatore o utente. La persona fisica che agisce per scopi estranei all'attività imprenditoriale o professionale eventualmente svolta' (Art. 3(1) *Codice del Consumo*).

a special protection of consumers has nonetheless proved the insufficiency of such formal protection. That is why Article 1341 CC is still in force and continues to be applied, even though in the particular area of consumer contracts its practical utility has been bypassed by the implementation of Directive EC/93/13 and the following adoption of Articles 1469*bis* et seq. CC, now replaced by Articles 33 et seq. *Codice del Consumo*.

80. Whereas Article 1341 CC only provides a formal protection for the party who adheres to the contract (principle of knowledge of the term notwithstanding its fairness) and it applies to commercial as well as to consumer contracts, a substantial protection especially dedicated to consumer contracts is also provided under the *Codice del Consumo*.

The unfair contract terms Directive EC/93/13 was in fact implemented in Italy in the Law of 6 February 1986 No. 52 which led to the introduction of CAPO XIV-*bis* entitled 'Consumer contracts' in the Civil Code.[63]

81. After a long discussion, a specific code for consumer law was approved in 2005: the former discipline set by Articles 1469*bis* and following CC has been 'transferred' into the said code, in order to create a 'priviledged' locus for consumer legislation. It is consequently Article 33 *Codice del Consumo* that now gives the definition of an unfair term (*clausola vessatoria*): a contractual term which has not been individually negotiated will be regarded as unfair if, contrary to the requirement of good faith, it causes a significant imbalance in the parties' rights and obligations arising under the contract, to the detriment of the consumer.

82. The same article also provides a list of clauses that are presumed to be unfair (so-called grey list). Except where there is proof to the contrary, such terms included in the list will be assumed to be unfair if they have the object or effect of:

(a) excluding or limiting the legal liability of a seller or supplier in the event of the death of a consumer or personal injury to the latter resulting from an act or omission of that seller or supplier;

---

63. See *also* the Ministerial Decree 19 Jan. 1999, No. 20 concerning procedures for registering on the list of Consumer's and Service Users Associations represented at a national level (published in the Official Gazette No. 29 of 5 Feb. 1999). The decree brings into being, from the Ministry of Industry's General Directorate for the Harmonization and Protection of the Market, lists of consumers and service users associations represented at a national level, specifying the enrolment procedure, based on the requirements of Art. 5 of the law of 30 Jul. 1998, No. 281; stabilizing the procedure for making additions to the list. Following the Ministerial Decree 20/1999 the circular 9 Mar. 1999, No. 12511 (published in the GU No. 71 of 26 Mar. 1999) defines the criteria and operating instructions for registering on the list of associations of consumers and service users at a national level. The circular was issued by the Ministry of Industry's General Directorate for the Harmonization and Protection of the Market, to supply clarifications and instructions to consumers and service users associations about the presentation of requests to be registered on the list, as laid out in Act 281/99 and maintained by the same General Directorate.

(b) inappropriately excluding or limiting the legal rights of the consumer *vis-à-vis* the seller or supplier or another party in the event of total or partial non-performance or inadequate performance by the seller or supplier of any of the contractual obligations;

(c) excluding or limiting objections by the consumer to the offsetting of a debt owed to the seller or supplier against any claim which the consumer may have against him/her;

(d) making an agreement binding on the consumer when provision of services by the seller or supplier is subject to a condition whose realization depends on his/her own will alone;

(e) permitting the seller or supplier to retain sums paid by the consumer where the latter decides not to conclude or perform the contract, without providing for the consumer to receive compensation of an equivalent amount from the seller or supplier where the latter is the party cancelling the contract;

(f) requiring any consumer who fails to fulfil his/her obligation in time to pay a disproportionately high sum in compensation;

(g) authorizing the seller or supplier to dissolve the contract on a discretionary basis where the same facility is not granted to the consumer, or permitting the seller or supplier to retain the sums paid for services not yet supplied by him/her where it is the seller or supplier himself/herself who dissolves the contract;

(h) enabling the seller or supplier to terminate a contract of indeterminate duration without reasonable notice except where there are serious grounds for doing so;

(i) automatically extending a contract of fixed duration where the consumer does not indicate otherwise, when the deadline fixed for the consumer to express this desire not to extend the contract is unreasonably early;

(j) irrevocably binding the consumer to terms with which he/she had no real opportunity of becoming acquainted before the conclusion of the contract;

(k) enabling the seller or supplier to alter the terms of the contract, or any characteristics of the product or service to be provided, unilaterally without a valid reason which is specified in the contract;

(l) providing for the price of goods or services to be determined at the time of delivery;

(m) allowing a seller of goods or supplier of services to increase its price without giving the consumer the corresponding right to cancel the contract if the final price is too high in relation to the price agreed when the contract was concluded;

(n) giving the seller or supplier the right to determine whether the goods or services supplied are in conformity with the contract, or giving him/her the exclusive right to interpret any term of the contract;

(o) limiting the seller's or supplier's obligation to respect commitments undertaken by his/her agents or making his/her commitments subject to compliance with a particular formality;

(p) excluding or limiting the consumer's freedom to raise objections in the event of non-performance;

(q) giving the seller or supplier the possibility of transferring his/her rights and obligations under the contract, even with the consumer's prior agreement, where this may serve to reduce the guarantees for the latter;

(r) imposing upon the consumer losses, restrictions on the right to raise objections, derogations to the competence of the legal authority, restrictions on the allegation of proof, reversal or amendment of the burden of proof and restrictions on contractual freedom in relations with third parties;

(s) stipulating a head office in a place other than that in which the consumer resides as the place of jurisdiction in the event of disputes;

(t) providing for the alienation of a right or the assumption of an obligation to be subject to a suspenseful condition depending solely upon the will of the seller or supplier, in contrast to an immediate obligation on the part of the consumer. This is without prejudice to the provisions of Article 1355 of the Civil Code.

One should note that the national implementing measures refer to all contracts relating to the sale of goods or provision of services here, included insurance contracts.

In particular, one should remember that if the purpose of the contract is to supply financial services of indeterminate duration, the supplier may, in derogation from items (h) and (k), cancel without notice, where there is a valid reason, provided that the consumer is informed thereof immediately; alter unilaterally, where there is a valid reason, the conditions of the contract, provided that the consumer is given reasonable notice and that the consumer is free to dissolve the contract.

83. Once again, if the purpose of the contract is to supply financial services, the supplier may alter the rate of interest payable by the consumer or due to the latter, or the amount of other charges for financial services, without notice where there is a valid reason, provided that he/she informs the consumer thereof immediately and that the latter has the right to dissolve the contract. Items (h) and (k)–(m) do not apply to contracts relating to transferable securities, financial instruments and other products or services where the price is linked to fluctuations in a stock exchange quotation or index or a financial market rate that the seller or supplier does not control, or to contracts for the purchase or sale of foreign currency, travellers' cheques or international money orders denominated in foreign currency. Items (l) and (m) are without hindrance to price-indexation clauses, where lawful, provided that the method by which prices vary is explicitly described.

84. Italian legislation accepted the principle established by Directive EC/93/13 that the 'core terms' of the contracts are not submitted to the so-called fairness test. That statement is in line with the principle that the judge may not interfere with the essential nature and duties assumed by the parties in the contracts. Consequently, under Article 34, I comma *Codice del Consumo*, assessing the unfair nature of a term bears no relation to the subject of the contract or to the fairness of the corresponding amount of goods and services. Nonetheless, the exemption of such clauses from the fairness test is relative as it operates provided these elements are clearly set out.[64]

---

64. The law of 6 Feb. 1996, No. 52 (Art. 25), Provisions for the fulfilment of obligations deriving from Italy's membership of the European Community – Community Law 1994, Official Gazette of the Italian Republic, 10 Feb. 1996, No. 24 SO. Comments can be read in Candian, Cerini and Petrone, 'Clausole vessatorie e contratti di assicurazione', in Alpa and Patti (eds.), *Le clausole vessatorie nei*

85. A principle of internal coherence of the legal system requires that terms which reproduce legal provisions, or repeat provisions or implement principles set out in international conventions to which the European Union and all its Member States are signatories, cannot be judged as unfair (so-called white list).

86. Terms or elements of terms which have been the subject of individual negotiation are not unfair. Besides, one should consider that the proof an individual negotiation is quite difficult to give. The approval of a single clause in writing is not relevant as a proof of individual negotiation. Besides, the case law has considered that if a contract is concluded by a public act in front of a notary individual negotiation has taken place.[65]

In any case, terms are considered not binding, even if they have been negotiated, if they have the object or effect of:

– excluding or limiting the legal liability of a seller or supplier in the event of the death of a consumer or personal injury to the latter resulting from an act or omission of that seller or supplier;
– excluding or limiting the legal rights of the consumer *vis-à-vis* the seller or supplier or another party in the event of total or partial non-performance or inadequate performance by the seller or supplier;
– irrevocably binding the consumer to terms with which he/she had no real opportunity of becoming acquainted before the conclusion of the contract.

This non-binding nature shall operate solely to the advantage of the consumer and may be overturned by the courts (so-called black list).

87. A special rule is provided by Article 34, last comma *Codice del Consumo* for the case of contracts stipulated on the basis of a pre-formulated form ('standard contracts'). In fact in standard form contracts the seller or supplier bears the burden of proof that the terms or elements thereof, despite having been pre-formulated by him/her, have been the subject of specific negotiation with the consumer.

In addition, in the case of contracts where all or certain terms offered to the consumer are in writing, these terms must always be drafted in plain, intelligible language (see Article 35, I *Codice del Consumo*). This provision appears as a special application of the principle of transparency.

Consistent with the traditional rule of the *interpretatio contra proferentem*, whenever there is any doubt about the meaning of a term, the interpretation most favourable to the consumer must prevail (Article 1469*quarter*, II comma – new rule Article 35, II *Codice del Consumo*).

88. Once a contract term has been declared unfair, the consequence is rather radical: terms considered unfair are invalid, while the rest of the contract remains in

---

contratti con i consumatori. Commentario agli articoli 1469bis – 1469sexies del Codice Civile, Milan, 1997; F. Romeo, *La tutela del consumatore nel contratto di assicurazione danni*, Milan, 2004.
65. See for an application Trib. Roma, 21 Jan. 2000, which can be read in *Foro It.*, 2000, I.

force. The seller or service supplier has the right of redress against the supplier for damages incurred as a result of unfair terms being declared void.

89. Article 36, last comma *Codice del Consumo* provides special rules if a choice of law is allowed. In this case, no contractual term will be binding if, in providing for the applicability to the contract of the legislation of a non-member country, it has the effect of depriving the consumer of the protection of this article, where the contract shows a closer link with the territory of a Member State of the European Union.

90. Consumer associations, professional associations, chambers of commerce, industry, crafts and agriculture may summon to court the seller or supplier or the professional association using general contract conditions and ask the competent judge to prohibit the use of terms deemed to be unfair within the meaning of this chapter. In particular, the courts have considered the National Association of Insurance Companies (ANIA) in such a position even through the association does not 'use' general conditions but recommends or suggests their application to Italian companies who are free to follow the suggestion or not.

91. An interim injunction may be granted where there are justified reasons for urgency. The applicable procedure is that provided by Articles 669(a) et seq. of the Code of Civil Procedure. In particular, the judge may order that the measure be published in one or more newspapers, of which at least one must have a national circulation. The purchaser may appeal through the normal legal channels on grounds of infringement of subjective rights, in order to obtain compensation for infringement of contractual obligations. Before legal proceedings begin, efforts will be made to settle out of court.

92. Since the entry into force of the unfair contract terms regulation established by Articles 1469*bis* et seq. of the Civil Code (now Codice del Consumo), a number of relevant clauses of insurance contracts have been considered not binding for consumers. In particular, the unfairness of the term has been declared with respect to the following:

– a clause establishing a derogation to the competent judiciary authority by conferring the power to decide over a judicial matter to arbitration judgment;[66] – a clause assessing the right of unilateral withdrawal of the insurer after the event insured occurs;
– a clause establishing a deadline of sixty or ninety days for the consumer to express the desire to avoid the extension of the contract duration.[67]

93. Following the implementation of Directive 93/13/EC and the development of a culture of transparency in insurer–consumer relations, the setting of an activity

---

66. See Trib. Torino, 15 Oct. 1996 with a partially dissenting opinion of scholars which can be read in *Giust civ.*, 1997, I, 1409.
67. Trib. Roma, 8 May 1998, in *Foro it.*, 98, I, 1989.

of constant renovation of insurance contract terms has been agreed between ANIA and the most representative consumer associations.

94.   In particular a letter of intent was signed on 11 May 1999 between ANIA, UEA (Unione Europea Assicurazioni) ADICONSUM ADOC, *Comitato Altroconsumo*, *Lega Consumatori ACLI*, *Movimento Consumatori* and the *Unione Nazionale Consumatori*. The text contains a number of suggestions and recommendations to the associations in order to introduce a fairer and balanced relation between the parties.

§4.   DUTY OF TRANSPARENCY AND INFORMATION

95.   The nineteenth century and the first half of the twentieth century have focused on the duties of information on the charge of the insured parties. In the second half of the twentieth century, until today, the opposite flows of information have been protagonists.

96.   Such a change of perspective is due to a change of perception about the asymmetric relationship between the insured party and insurers. The original idea that the insured was the one that best appreciated the risk has not disappeared; nonetheless, when we talk about imbalance of information in contracts with consumers, we take a realistic view, accepting that the contractor does not read the contractual content and therefore does not know it; even if he/she did, he/she would not be able to appreciate the content in the way the other party would, therefore subscribing behind a veil of ignorance.

The persuasive strength of this assumption is noticeable, and it has highlighted as much the disclosure duties of companies as those of intermediaries, as far as the content of the contractual text is concerned.

The importance of the duty of information of the insured is clearly testified by the *Codice delle Assicurazioni Private* where a complete title (Titolo XIII) deals with the duties of information and transparency towards the insured. More rules are set by ISVAP Regulation no.35/2010 on the information obligations and the advertising of insurance products.

97.   The need of protection of the consumer through transparency and information finds an answer in the duty to give maximum information prior to the conclusion of the contract. In particular, a first level of transparency in consumer contracts is granted by the duty to give the insured the Information Dossier; the Dossier must contain the Information notice (*nota informative)*, the proposal of insurance, where used, and the full text of contract terms (*condizioni di contratto*). Isvap also requires that a glossary is included in the Information Dossier to be given prior to the conclusion of the contract.

Of the said documents included in the Dossier, the information notice is the one that has mostly innovated the practice of insurers. In fact, since 1995, the information notice is a document that the insurer is obliged to give to the consumer before the conclusion of the contract (the duty was first introduced by the Legislative Decrees 174-175/1995. The relevant rule is now Article 185 CAP).

The specific content of the information notice is integrated, in life and non-life insurance, by specific regulation set by ISVAP and it provides for information useful in order to identify the insurance company, the basic elements of the contract, the clauses of exclusion, etc.[68]

98. Even more recently, first with the Circular Letter 533/D/2004, ISVAP had introduced stricter rules concerning information to be given to consumers through the Internet and with reference to the means of payment allowed. In particular, following Circular Letter 533/D/2004 of ISVAP, all insurance companies operating in Italy were obliged to publish on the web all information notices and contract terms relative to the offered products in order to permit comparability between offers on the market and to ensure better information for consumers and financial services users.

99. In addition, under Circular Letter 551/D/2005 of ISVAP, applicable to life insurance contracts, insurance companies and insurance intermediaries were obliged to give the client proper information according to his/her needs and to keep reports of all answers given. This duty, which anticipated those provided by the Second Directive on insurance intermediaries (Directive EC/2002/92), are now part of Title IX of the *Codice delle Assicurazioni Private.*[69]

100. As anticipated, with Regulation 35/2010, the Control Authority has strengthen the duties if information for both life and non-life insurance contracts. In particular, the Reg.35/2010 requires the insurance companies to deliver, prior to the conclusion of the contract, an Information Dossier (in Italian Fascicolo Informativo). The Information Dossier is intended to be a 'package' where the consumer and other clients can find all information and rules concerning the insurance contracts they are going to enter into. According to many commentators, nevertheless, the Information Dossier is too redundant as the large number of information to be given to the consumer and clients in general will not truly increase their comprehension of the contract, but only increase cost of insurance. For this reason, a 'movement' for the simplifying of documents and information requirement is on the way and the table of discussion with the institutions and regulators is open.

§5. THE PROTECTION OF PERSONAL DATA: THE PRIVACY CODE

101. Personal data protection law finds its origins in the Republican Constitution of 1948 and has remarkably accelerated thanks to the special care given to the matter in an international context.

---

68. Corte Appello di Roma, 7 May 2002, with comment in *Danno e Responsabilità*, 2002, 966.
69. For models and schemes of the information notice in the different lines of insurance see annexes to the ISVAP regulation 35/2010.

Article 14 of the Constitution states the fundamental right to protect the individual from inspection and verification of personal data and correspondence. A number of criminal laws give special protection with reference to specific offences such as violation of personal mail, investigation of private activities, and so on.

On the other hand, leading cases by civil law courts set basic principles in order to protect the image and reputation of the individual and in the direction of recognizing fair compensation in the case of violation.

Despite the existing rules and the attention of the courts, in practical terms the protection of personal data was quite fragmented and the right to personal privacy was never assumed as a general right.

102. It was only in 1996, after twenty years of debate, that Legislative Decree No. 675 was approved. It was the first systematic attempt to give a complete discipline protecting personal data and, more in general privacy.

This discipline was considerably amended by Legislative Decree No. 467/2001 and finally substituted by a Legislative Decree of 2003 representing the Code of Personal Data (or Privacy Code).

As a result of these acts, a board of experts named *Garante della privacy* (simply the *Garante*) entrusted with special tasks and duties was set up with the aim of monitoring data protection. The board is made up of four members elected by both parliamentary houses and a fifth member elected by the others. Failure to comply with measures taken by the *Garante* is a criminal offence.

103. The actual legislation points out some fundamental principles concerning data protection. In particular, all personal data must be processed lawfully and fairly; they can only be recorded for specific, explicit and legitimate purposes. Collected personal data must not be kept for longer period that is necessary for the purposes for which the data were collected (*diritto all'oblio*).

A fundamental distinction is made by the law between the controller of the data (*titolare*) and the processor of the data (*responsabile*), who is the person appointed by the controller to process data on his/her behalf.

In order to collect or process personal data, the consent of the person involved is strictly necessary. Sensitive personal data, such as that related to sex, religion, health, racial or ethnic origin, political opinions, benefit from a greater degree of protection. According to this set of rules, all insurance companies, intermediaries and experts who collect and process personal data have to collect the necessary consent of their clients or third parties and to treat the data fairly, in particular ensuring protection against undue interference.

Part II. The Insurance Contract: General

Chapter 1. Classification of Insurance Activities and Insurance Contracts

104. Classification of insurance activities may proceed upon numerous and different bases. A first and fundamental classification in law is between life insurance and non-life insurance. Legislative Decrees No. 174/1995 and No. 175/1995 implemented the third European directives and introduced the division into six branches for life insurance (Article 2 of *Codice Assicurazione Private* or CAP).

When distinguishing between life and non-life insurance activities, the legislator did not intend to make reference to a corresponding distinction between legal types of contracts and nor was the insurance contract assumed as a basis for the distinction. The aim of the distinction is in fact for public purposes to regulate access to insurance activities and the release of the necessary authorizations.

105. When carrying on the activities scheduled under branches 1–6 of the life-insurance business or 1–18 of non-life insurance business, insurance companies can offer contracts that do not belong to the legal (or named) type of insurance as regulated by Articles 1882 et seq. of the Civil Code. This is the case, for example, with suretyship, capitalization policies and pension funds.

This clarification is essential in order to understand the functioning of the Italian legal system: as a civil law country, the conceptual approach to contract law requires the interpreter to identify whether a contract is a typical (or named) one. If this is the case, the general rules of contracts apply if they do not conflict with the specific rules set for the individual contract at issue.[70] If the agreement entered into by the parties is qualified as an insurance contract, the general principles of contract law (Articles 1321 et seq. CC) are applicable where not derogated from by the special rules set by Articles 1882–1932 CC.

106. It can be inferred from the wording of Article 1882 CC that private law makes a fundamental distinction between insurance contracts against damages (*assicurazioni contro i danni*), where the insurer compensates the insured for damage

---

70. See further below, Part VI.

caused by an accident, and life insurance contracts (*assicurazione sulla vita*) where the insurer pays a sum – or annuity – upon an event related to the human life.

Taking this basic distinction, Articles 1882 CC–1903 CC set general rules applicable to all insurance contracts. Articles 1904 CC–1918 CC are applicable only to contracts against damages (*assicurazione danni*). Articles from 1919 CC to 1931 CC refer to life insurance contracts only. Article 1932 CC is a general rule enumerating the clauses which cannot be derogated from by the parties and it is consequently applicable to all contracts of insurance.

107. It is worth remembering that the distinction between life insurance contracts and contracts against damages does not completely coincide with that between indemnity and non-indemnity contracts. In fact, the latter distinction derives from a speculative activity of the legal doctrine, in order to establish the application of the general principles concerning the nature of the interest of the insured and the rules referring to the indemnity principle.

From a legal point of view, a contract against damages to persons is not a life insurance contract. Therefore, it should be submitted to all the rules concerning such contracts, including the duty of salvage (Article 1915 CC) and the indemnity principle (Article 1908 CC).

Nonetheless, given the particular nature of the risk connected with the human life, legal doctrine discourages the plain and simple application of the rules concerning non-life insurance to personal damage insurance (i.e., *assicurazione infortuni*) as well as to some forms of illness insurance (*assicurazione malattia*).

On the assumption that personal damage insurance is not fully included in the indemnity contracts category, this critical approach is shared by part of the case-law that makes use of the analogical process in order to extend the application of the principles and rule governing life insurance to other insurances of the person.[71]

108. Another important distinction at law is made between marine and non-marine (or terrestrial) insurance contracts.

Marine insurance finds its main discipline in the Code of Navigation and it may be regarded as a sui generis section of insurance contracts.[72] In fact, Article 1885 CC states that marine insurance is governed by the provisions of the Civil Code concerning terrestrial insurance insofar as it is not differently regulated by the Code of Navigation.

All other forms of insurance are governed by Articles 1882 et seq. of the Civil Code.

---

71. A.M. Musy & A. Monti, 'Contract Law I', in *Introduction to Italian law*, ed. J.S. Lena-UMattei, 247–282.
72. See Cass. 66/2336; Cass. 71/1941.

Chapter 2. Definition and General Characteristics of the Insurance Contract: A Typical Contract

109. In the Italian legal system, the contract of insurance is a typical (or nominate), bilateral and consensual contract. Each of these phrases needs a proper explanation.

It should first be remembered that Italian law offers a definition of contract as 'the agreement between two or more parties to create, regulate or terminate an economic legal relationship' (Article 1321 CC). This definition not only stresses the economic relevance of the contractual agreements, including the insurance contract, but it also introduces, in combination with Article 1322 CC, the fundamental principle of the freedom of contract.

In particular, once the power of the parties to enter into an agreement for the regulation or termination of an economic legal relationship creation is recognized, Article 1322 CC focuses on the so-called *autonomia contrattuale* (*libertà contrattuale* or freedom of contract).

110. The notion of freedom of contract has different applications. In a very general sense, freedom of contract means that each person is free to enter or not to enter into a contract. This principle suffers a limitation in insurance law with reference to the bilateral duty to be insured and to insure in motor liability insurance.[73]

In a second meaning, the freedom of contract is to be intended as the right of the parties to freely determine the content of the contract within the limit imposed by the law (Article 1322 CC, I comma).

In an even wider sense, freedom of contract allows the party to conclude unnamed or atypical contracts, provided that these contracts are directed to the realization of interests worthy of protection according to the legal order (Article 1322 CC, II comma).

Within the field of insurance, this freedom has been often applied, provided that the only limit for the parties is to conclude contracts included in the notion of insurance activities corresponding to one of the branches for public authorization.

111. In addition to the general principles of contract law, special rules apply to the contract of insurance which is in fact a typical (or nominate) contract. The typical or (nominate) character of the insurance contract derives from the fact that its essential features are established by law and in particular by Article 1882 CC.[74]

Here the contract of insurance is defined as:

> a contract whereby one party, the insurer, on the payment of premium, binds himself to compensate the insured, within the limit agreed upon, for damages caused to the insured by an accident, or to pay a principal sum or annuity upon the happening of an event upon human life.[75]

---

73. See for a complete analysis S. Ferrarini, *Le assicurazioni marittime*, 3rd edn (Milan, 1991).
74. See below, Part III.
75. For the concept of nominate or typical contract in Italian legislation see A.M. Musy & A. Monti, 'Contract law' in *Introduction to Italian Law,* ed. J.S. Lena & U. Mattei (Kluwer, 2002), 247ff.

112. Despite its importance for the description of the principal duties of the parties (payment of premiums against payment of a certain sum in terms of compensation, or capital, or annuity) the above-mentioned legal definition of insurance does not seem to offer an exhaustive description of the essential elements of the insurance contract. Additional elements were later expressed by judicial decisions and analyses formulated by legal doctrine. It is indeed from judicial pronouncements and from comments by the legal doctrine that the observer can discern certain characteristics that, even if unexpressed by the legal definition, are nevertheless fully compatible with it.[76]

113. Stating that the legal definition of the insurance contract may not be sufficiently comprehensive, some authors have asserted that the essential element of insurance is the transfer of the risk or, even more precisely, the economic consequence of the risk, to the insurer.[77] The insurable risk is that of an event which is in the future and uncertain. The risk may be that of an event of damage or an event related to the life of the insured person.

114. With reference to the duty of the insurer, legal doctrine has proposed to interpret the terms of Article 1882 CC so that not only capital sums or indemnities can be paid by the insurer (the latter being expressly mentioned by Article 1882 CC). The parties are consequently free to establish that the duty of the insurer may also consist of offering collateral services (i.e., legal services or other forms of assistance) if a detrimental event occurs.

---

76. As translated by Beltramo, *The Italian Civil Code*, 2001.
77. It is important to clarify that the analysis, in terms of essential elements of the contract, is necessary in order to identify the agreements to which the legal provisions concerning insurance applies, and to clarify the extent and limits of insurance activity which is strictly limited to the offer of insurance contracts and the other insurance activities expressly named by Art. 2 CAP).

Chapter 3. The Formation of the Insurance Contract

115. The contract of insurance is no exception to the general rule requiring that all contracts must have the following fundamental elements: agreement between the parties (*accordo*), the *causa*,[78] the object (*oggetto*) and the form (*forma*) where prescribed by law, under the sanction of nullity of the contract (Article 1325 CC).

116. The contract of insurance is no exception either to the general principle of contract law under which the formation of a valid agreement has to be based on an offer by one party and acceptance by the other, as provided by Article 1326 CC.[79]

This rule expresses the traditional view of the contract as an agreement between two parties based on mutual consent. The mutual consent does not have to be in writing. In fact, the basic principle of Italian law is that the intention and consent of the parties can be expressed in any way they wish unless a specific form is required by law or agreed upon by the parties.

Performance is considered to equivalent to the expression of consent (Article 1327 CC). The rule is applied to insurance contracts where the premium paid is immediately invested in funds.

117. The offer to enter into an insurance contract can be made by a prospective insured or by the insurer. In practical terms it is mostly considered that the prospective insured is the one who makes the proposal, regardless of the fact that he/she is often solicited by the insurer or by his/her agents to enter the insurance agreement.

More generally, the prospective insured may fill in a standard proposal form made by the insurer. After receiving the complete proposal form, the insurer can simply accept or may accept with qualifications, in which case the acceptance is considered a counter offer (Article 1326 CC, last comma). The contract will come into being when the party to whom the offer is made accepts it unconditionally and the acceptance reaches the offering party.

If the contract is intermediated by the broker, the acceptance of the insurer made to the broker is effective with regard to the insured when the mandate conferred by the client on the broker provides for a power to receive contractual declarations.

118. According to Article 1887 CC, a written offer to the insurer is irrevocable for a period of fifteen days or for a longer period of thirty days when a medical examination is necessary. This period has effect from the date of delivery or from the date of the mailing of the offer.

---

78. G. Scalfi, *Manuale delle assicurazioni private* (Milan, 1994).
79. Despite its importance as one of the essential element of a contract, the *causa* is not defined by law and the notion is quite controversial. It seems wise to assume in this monograph the two main concepts of the *causa*. The objective perspective defines the *causa* as the typical social and economic function of the contract. The subjective perspective defines the *causa* as the aim pursued by the party in undertaking the obligations (see for a deeper analysis Musy and Monti, *supra*).

It is better to specify that this rule was initially applicable to all insurance contracts. Following the implementation of the third Life European Directive by Legislative Decree No. 175/1995, the principle of the irrevocable offer by the prospective insured was implicitly abrogated for life insurance contracts.

The *Codice delle Assicurazioni Private* has reproduced the rule in Article 176 but once again no reference to coordination with Article 1887 has been made.

Chapter 4. Duration, Renewal and Effect of Insurance Coverage

119. On the premises, the parties are free to establish the duration of the insurance contract. Nonetheless, in order to protect them against duties that may last for too long, if the duration of the contract exceeds ten years, after the expiry of this period the parties – regardless of agreements to the contrary – can withdraw from the contract with six-months' notice, which can also be given by means of a registered letter (Article 1899 CC, I comma).

It should be noted that in fact insurance contracts offered in the Italian market generally do not exceed the five-year term, unless for life insurance and insurance of the persons where a longer term is essential for the nature of the risk.

120. An insurance contract can be tacitly renewed or extended one or more times, but each tacit extension cannot exceed the duration of two years (Article 1899 CC, II comma).

121. A practical but important rule provided by law is that insurance is effective from midnight of the day on which the contract was entered into to midnight of the last day of the period stipulated in the contract (Article 1899 CC, I comma), if the first insurance premium has been paid. Nonetheless, it is quite common for the insurance agreement to specify that the insurance coverage will not be effective until a specific requirement has been complied with, e.g., the completion of a medical examination.

122. The rules set out by Article 1899 CC are not applicable to life insurance contracts which are regulated under Article 1924 CC.[80]

---

80. A contract is formed at the time when the person who made the offer has knowledge of the acceptance of the other party (Art. 1326 CC).

Chapter 5. Formalities of the Insurance Contract

123. In the Italian legal system as well as in all modern ones, no particular form is generally required for the manifestation of an intention if not specifically required by law.

When the law generally speaks about the adoption of a specific form for declaration or agreements, a fundamental distinction is to be set between the form necessary for the validity of the declaration or the agreement (so-called *forma ad substantiam*) and the form necessary for the proof of the agreement (*forma ad probationem* or evidentiary formality).

124. In the first case – *forma ad substantiam* – the specific form prescribed by the law is an essential element of the contract, so that the validity of the contract is submitted to the adoption of that special form (this may be a simple written form or a public act or even the solemn form required by the law).

In the second case – *forma ad probationem* – the contract is valid even if it does not comply with the written form; failure to comply with the required form affects the law of evidence. The reason for the adoption of evidentiary formalities is connected with the need for certainty.

The distinction between the two situations (*forma ad substantiam or ad probationem*) is not always expressly stated by the law but it can be inferred by the type of sanction connected to the lack of the prescribed form.

125. According to Italian law, the insurance contract is a consensual one so that it can be validly stipulated in any form, which is to say oral form or written form. This means that even an oral agreement is valid, perfect and binding at law:[81] this is a consequence of the qualification in terms of *contratto consensuale* (consensual contract) where no *forma ad substantiam* is required.

126. If the insurance contract can validly exist even if entered into by oral agreement, in practical terms the oral stipulation is a true exception. This statement is sustained by several examples.

First of all, in practice the stipulation of insurance agreements in oral form is reduced by the rule set by Article 1888 CC. This provides that a contract of insurance be evidenced in writing. The document is generally called *polizza* (policy), and contains the signature of the insured and the insurer.[82] After the joint signature, the insurer is bound to deliver to the policyholder the insurance policy and other documents signed by him/her. Moreover, at the request and expense of the policyholder, he/she is bound to deliver duplicates or copies of the policy (in this case, the original should be returned, if it is not lost).[83]

---

81. See below, Part IV.
82. See Gambino, *Contratto di assicurazione. Profili generali, Enciclopedia Giuridica*, III, 12.
83. It goes without saying that different documents are able to prove the existence of the contract. In maritime insurance the policy is substituted by a so-called *certificato di sicurtà*. The policy can also be written after the conclusion of the contract (Cass. 15 Mar. 1966 No. 750).

These rules clearly show that the use of the written form for probation represents a protection for the policyholder, who may need to hand in the written documents in order to take action against a bad-faith insurer. At the same time, the insurer may need the written form in order to prove the limits and exclusion of the policy.

It has to be clarified, nevertheless, that the requirement of the written form only applies to the content of the policy and not to its existence, which may be proved by any means.

Following the application of the general rules on probation, the existence of the contract may be proven by testifying if the party, without any fault, lost the documents that provided the evidence (Article 2724, No. 3 CC).[84]

127. Another limitation to the stipulation of insurance contracts in oral form relates to specific duties of information and disclosure of the insurer towards the insured. In fact, even if no specific rule exists with reference to contracts concluded by consumers, in practical terms the duty of the insurer to give preliminary information in writing eliminates the possibility of stipulating standard oral contracts with consumers.

128. In any case, the written form is required for a number of acts and situations concerning the life of the insurance contract and the relation between the insurer and his/her counterparts.

In fact, the adoption of the written form as well as the signature by the insured or policyholder is required, at least in the following cases:

- for the specific acceptance of standard conditions provided by Article 1341 of the Civil Code;
- for the consent of the third party whose life the contract is concluded on (Article 1919 of the Civil Code); – for the policyholder's declaration that he/she has been given due information notice on paper, or other durable medium, before the conclusion of the contract, as required by Article 185 CAP); – for the statements made by the policyholder under Articles 1892–1893 of the Civil Code on the risk to be insured.

129. Finally, it should be remarked that the parties can introduce specific formalities into the contract. In particular, the parties can bind the conclusion of the contract to the issuing of the policy schedule, which is written.

This agreement must be inserted in the proposal form and not in further documents.[85]

---

84. See A.D. Candian, *Forma e assicurazione* (Milan, 1988). The insurer can refuse to release the policy if the insured has failed to pay the premium (Cass. 31 Jan. 1967 No. 285, with comment in Ass., 1968, II, 201).
85. Cass. 29 Mar. 1993 No. 3771, in NGC, 1994, I, 184.

Chapter 6. Construction and Interpretation of the Insurance Contract

§1. General Rules Concerning the Construction of Contracts

130. Although the insurance contract is (or should be) the result of mutual consent and free determination by the parties, the way in which they express their will may give rise to uncertainties in the interpretation during the course of its execution. Consequently, despite the need to respect the parties' will, according to the so-called principle of sanctity of the contract, its clauses and terms may be (and often are) submitted to judicial interpretation.

131. The systematic application of the rules set out by the Civil Code on the matter of construction and interpretation of the contracts leads to the conclusion that for a nominated contract – such as an insurance contract – general contract rules are applicable if not derogated and as long as they do not conflict with eventual special rules set with reference to the nominated contract, so that general rules for the construction and interpretation of contracts set by Articles 1362 et seq. provided by Book IV of the Civil Code are fully applicable to insurance contracts provided that no specific discipline exists in insurance.

It is useful to remember that the Civil Code rules on interpretation can be distinguished in two main groups of articles. The first group collects provisions that tend to ascertain the intention of the party (so-called *regole di interpretazione soggettiva*) – Articles 1362–1365 CC – while the second group relates to provisions aiming at establishing the objective meaning of the contract (*regole di interpretazione oggettiva*) – Articles 1367–1371 CC (between them is the *contra proferentem* rule discussed below).

132. The first group (Articles 1362–1365 CC) is to be considered prevalent, as the articles tend to give the historic interpretation of the contract and to discover the concrete intention of the parties. The second group of rules (Articles 1367–1371 CC) applies only if the common intention of the parties could not be ascertained.

In practical terms, the courts – making a discretionary use of the voluntary principle – tend to mix the two systems and to apply the rule according to which the words in a policy are to be given their literal meaning unless a different meaning was understood by the parties when the contract was made.

At the intersection of the two hermeneutic sets of rules stands Article 1366 CC according to which the contract has to be interpreted in good faith terms. This general clause could have a strong impact on the interpretation of insurance contracts but it is seldom used by the judges.

§2. The Contra Proferentem Rule and Its Application in Insurance

133. Insurance contracts are most often standard or adhesion contracts. The rule of *in dubio interpretatio contra proferentem* established by Article 1370 CC is consequently often applied.

134. According to the above-mentioned rule (also abbreviated as the in *contra proferentem* rule) provisions contained in the standard conditions of a contract or in forms or formularies which have been prepared by one of the contracting parties, are interpreted, in case of doubt, in favour of the other party. If there is any ambiguity in the language used, the *contra proferentem* rule results in the adoption of the construction most favourable to the insured.[86]

It should be clarified that the notion of 'ambiguity' is applied by the courts in a very wide sense and may derive not only from the language of a single clause but also from a systematic reading of a number of clauses.

The decision Tribunale Milano, 10 gennaio 1994, *Soc. Lloyd adriatico c. Impr. Milone Edil*,[87] settled that:

> In un contratto di assicurazione della responsabilità civile è legittimamente applicato l'art. 1370 c.c. quando l'elevato numero di clausole non agevolmente coordinabili tra di loro, la varietà del loro contenuto, nonché l'uso incostante della punteggiatura siano idonei ad ingenerare dubbi nel contraente per adesione il quale sia portata in buona fede ad intendere le clausole nel significato a lui più favorevole.

135. If the contracting party is a consumer, the general rule of *contra proferentem interpretation* set by Article 1370 CC is strengthened by the discipline on unfair contract terms and in particular by Article 35 *Codice del Consumo*. The rules contained in the Codice del Consumo are set for consumer contracts and our case law has denied an extension of their application to non-expert professionals or small businesses.[88]

In fact, Article 35 *Codice del Consumo* provides for a duty of the professional to use a clear and comprehensible language. In particular, it stipulates that in the case of contracts in which all clauses or certain clauses are submitted to the consumer in writing, the clauses must always be drawn up in a clear and comprehensible manner. In case of doubt as to the meaning of a clause, the interpretation most favourable to the consumer prevails.

The rule is applicable only to contracts concluded after 1 January 1996 or to the actual effects of those concluded before.

---

86. See Donati, Volpe & Putzolu, *Manuale delle assicurazioni private* (Milan, 138).
87. Tribunale Melfi, 8 Mar. 1999 (*Soc. Zurigo assicur. c. Montanarella*), *Giur. merito* 2000, 1231, with observations by Mastromartino.
88. See the full text in *DEA*, 1995, 553.

Chapter 7. The Notion of Insurable Interest and the Indemnity Principle

136. The existence of an insurable interest is a strict and basic requirement of the insurance contract. It is important to realize that insurable interest is the particular relation that is established between the insured and the protected life of the property. This interest is not only present in case of a position of ownership of the contracting party with the insured property, but can be identified in any legally recognized insurance relationship consequent to which the policyholder can suffer a prejudice for the loss of the property or a benefit by its safety.[89]

137. According to Article 1904 CC, a contract of insurance of property and, more in general, an indemnity contract, is void if, at the time of the beginning of the insurance, the insured has no interest in the property for which he/she may be compensated in case of damage. The same rule is a fundamental basis in order to verify whether the indemnity principle was respected at the time of the conclusion of the contract.

---

89. See *also supra*, Ch. 2 on unfair contract terms in consumer contracts.

Chapter 8. Statutory and Contractual Rights to Amend the Contract during Its Term of Validity

§1. STATUTORY RIGHTS

138. A fundamental principle of general contract law is that it is forbidden for one party to introduce unilateral alteration or modification to premiums, contract terms or provisions, because of the well known and commonly accepted principle of *pacta sunt servanda* provided by the combined application of Articles 1321–1372 CC.

139. In addition, specific provisions of law tend to limit the validity of contractual clauses that have the effect of introducing a unilateral right to modify contract terms. Important references are those of Codice del Consumo, Articles 33 et seq. Those articles have replaced Articles 1469*bis* et seq. of the Civil Code implementing EC Directive 93/13 on unfair contract terms (i.e., the Codice del Consumo provides that clauses having as their object, or possibly resulting in, allowing the professional to unilaterally amend the contract clauses or the characteristics of the products or service supplied without a justifiable reason indicated in the contract, are unfair).[90]

140. Within the limit set by the Unfair Contract Terms Directive, the parties are free to introduce some clauses that have the effect of providing a unilateral right to modify the contract.

In practice, this power is used only with reference to the alteration of the premium at the end of the annual period and within specific limits. Such limits are clearly and specifically set in the contract itself independently from the will of the insurer (i.e., index rating alteration of the premium or the adjustment of the premium, as a consequence of the variation of the insured value). Technically speaking, in any case, these are not unilateral modification clauses because the criteria and effects of the alteration have been fully agreed by the parties at the time of the conclusion of the contract and no discretionary right to modify is given to the insurer.

Only in life insurance can companies introduce specific rights to modify some terms of the coverage within the period of validity of the contract and without the approval of the insured with specific reference to changes in mortality schedules. The supervisory authority has nevertheless required a particular procedure in order to ensure the right to information of the insured.

---

90. See Buttaro, *L'interesse nell'assicurazione* (Milan, 1954); Donati, *Trattato delle assicurazioni private*, II (Milan, 1954); Scalfi, *I contratti di assicurazione. L'assicurazione danni* (Turin, 1991).

§2. Contractual Right to Modify the Contract at Renewal

141. Within the general problem of modifying contract clauses, the alteration of contract clauses and premiums at the annual renewal of the contract is quite debatable because of the possible interpretation of the alteration itself as a proposal for a new contract. In other words, according to some scholars and interpreters, in case of alteration at the time of the renewal a new and full agreement would be necessary. This is coherent with the practice of most Italian insurance companies who give brand new contract documents to the insured in the case of 'renewal' with alteration.

In any case, in order to ensure equal protection to all consumers independently of the attitude of the single insurance company, the clause allowing the insurer to modify the premium or the contract terms in the case of automatically prolonged contracts has to provide at least that:

(a) the insured is adequately informed about the proposed alteration of the premium or about the variation in the contract terms before the expiry of the contract. For some lines of insurance (i.e., motor insurance) the supervisory authority and, later on, the law have fixed special rules concerning the time and ways in which the information has to be given;
(b) the insured has a right to terminate the contract, even if the contractual term for the exercise of the right of termination is expired. That means that the insured can decide not to accept the new conditions and terms until the last day of coverage and consequently to avoid the 'renewal';
(c) the new conditions will be applied only in case of express acceptance by the insured. The force of this rule is mitigated by the rule of implied acceptance or acceptance by performance (*comportamento concludente* o *accettazione per inizio dell'esecuzione* – see Articles 1327 et seq. CC entitled *esecuzione prima della risposta dell'accettante*, i.e., the payment of the new premium means acceptance of the same; if the alteration concerns the contract terms, a signature to the appendix containing the new clauses is required).

A specific agreement is not required only if the clause exactly defines the alteration (i.e., the same rule of the alteration during the validity of the contract, i.e., a clause of index rating of the premium).

§3. A Special Case of 'Modification': The Power to Terminate the Contract after Occurrence of an Insured Event

142. Before Directive EC/93/13 on unfair contract terms in insurance contracts, the majority of the policies used in the Italian market contained a clause of unilateral right of termination in favour of the insurer after the occurrence of an insured event.

After the implementation of the directive, a unilateral right of termination was no longer acceptable, as it would determine a significance imbalance of rights and duties of the parties in contrast with the good faith principle.

One of two alternatives is possible: (a) otherwise the clause is bilateral; in this case, the premium has to be given back to the insured if the insurer uses the right of termination or (b) there is no right of termination for either of the parties.

143. No special rule is provided for personal insurance. This is strongly criticized and, frankly, unacceptable as the balance between rights and duties of the parties is not automatically reintroduced with the simple transformation of a unilateral right in a bilateral one.

In any case, most Italian insurance companies have spontaneously erased the clause providing for a right of withdrawal (even bilateral) only for a short period of insurance has passed or have simply transformed long contracts into one-year contracts.

Chapter 9. The Duty to Pay the Premium

144. The payment of the premium is the main obligation on the charge of the undertaking.

The Italian system accepts the principle of indivisibility of the premium. This principle is well established and dates back to the Code of Commerce of 1882 with many practical applications.

145. If a contracting party fails to pay the premium, or the first instalment of the premium, insurance coverage is suspended until midnight of the day on which that contracting party pays the amount due (Article 1901 CC). In other words, there is a general rule that a contract of insurance does not come into force if the first premium is not paid, even if, in principle, the contract itself is valid and the insurer can sue to obtain the payment.

146. If the party fails to pay any subsequent premium at the maturity dates agreed upon, the insurance is suspended from midnight of the fifteenth day following the date of maturity. In the instances mentioned above, the contract is resolved by operation of law if the insurer within six-months from the maturity date of the premium or the instalment does not bring an action for collection; the insurer is only entitled to payment of the premium covering the current period of insurance and to reimbursement for expenses.

Where the premium is payable periodically, the policy is renewable with duty to pay an additional premium, it is the practice of insurers or their agents to send the insured reminder notices. Nonetheless, a failure to send out such a notice has no legal consequences according to the law. In principle, this can be evaluated according to the general duty of acting with utmost good faith but, in practice, the courts have never applied this principle to the matter.

147. These provisions do not apply to life insurance, for which Article 1924 CC provides special rules. In particular, Article 1924 CC establishes that if the party fails to pay the premium for the first year, the insurer can – within six months from the date of maturity of the premium – bring an action to obtain performance of the contract. This provision applies even if payment of the premium is divided into more than one instalment, always subject to the provisions of Article 1901 CC; in this case, the six-month period begins from the date of maturity of each instalment.

If the contracting party fails to pay the subsequent premiums within the period of grace provided by the policy, or in the absence of such provision, within twenty days from the date of maturity, the contract is dissolved by law. In this case, the premiums already paid to the insurer are retained, unless the conditions exist for redemption or reduction of the insurance contract.

Chapter 10. Utmost Good Faith and Duties of Disclosure in Insurance Contracts

§1. UTMOST GOOD FAITH IN GENERAL

148. The paramount obligation upon the parties to a contract is to act and behave according to the principle of good faith (Articles 1175, 1375 CC).[91] This obligation is considered at its highest level when related to the insurance contract, where each of the contractors has to observe utmost-good-faith towards the other. This obligation affects both the pre-contractual disclosure duties and activities and the execution of the contract for all its duration.

If one now moves from the duty of disclosure as an application of the utmost good faith rule, one should observe that in principle the duty of disclosure is a mutual one, required from both insurer and insured. In practice, the obligation rarely touches the insurer. Moreover, given the fact that the Italian courts are quite reluctant to apply general rules – such as the one of utmost good faith – only the duties of disclosure of the insured are specified in the Civil Code, and this determines the rare application of the utmost-good-faith rule to the charge of the insurer.

§2. DUTY TO DECLARE

149. A first application of the rule of utmost good faith relates to the pre-contractual duty of declaration. According to Italian legal provisions, the declaration of the risk must be complete, true and correct. These elements can be inferred by the combined letters of Articles 1892–1893 CC that sanction fraudulent, incorrect and incomplete declarations with a specific distinction between cases in which the declarations are made with fraud or gross negligence (Article 1892 CC) and cases in which declarations are made without fraud or gross negligence (Article 1893 CC).

150. The Italian legal system does not apply the model of the so-called guided declaration, which would have instead the effect of limiting the extent of the duty of declaration on the charge of the insured. In fact, the combined application of Articles 1892–3 CC builds a system where the insured has to know what a prudent insurer would like to know about the risk and consequently has to specify every element relevant for the evaluation of the risk. This rule has in principle the aim of reducing the so-called imbalance of knowledge between the parties, but everyone can understand how many practical problems it creates, especially when applied to the consumer who may not know which elements should be declared to the insured at the time of the conclusion of the contract.

---

91. The rule does not apply to contracts having as their object securities, financial instruments and other products or services whose price is connected with the floating of quotations and of a stock exchange index or a financial market rate which is not controlled by the professional, or the purchase and sale of foreign currency, travellers cheques or international money orders issued in foreign currency.

151. As a consequence, the national courts have tried to limit the extent of the duty of disclosure by applying a reversal in the burden of the proof on the charge of the insurer. They provide that when the prospective insured is required to complete a questionnaire prepared by the insurer, it is the responsibility of the insurer to prove that the elements not required in the questionnaire are relevant for the evaluation of the risk and the non-disclosure by the insured consequent to the insurance contract.

152. In the case of non-disclosure or wrongful declaration by the insured, two different types of consequences apply taking into consideration the case of intention or gross negligence of the insured or the case of simple negligence. In fact, if the omission or wrongful declaration is supported by intention or gross negligence of the insured, the insurer has the right to ask for the contract to be declared null and void when the insurer would not have given the consent or would have given consent on different conditions knowing the true circumstances.

The insurer forfeits his/her right to attack the contract if, within three months from the day of the knowledge, he/she fails to notify the contracting party of his/her intention to do so.

153. The insurer is entitled to the premiums covering the period of insurance running at the time the declaration of annulment is made and in all cases to premiums agreed upon for the first year. If an accident occurs before the expiration of the period indicated the insurer is not bound to pay (Article 1892 CC).

If the contracting party has acted without fraud or gross negligence, misrepresentations or failure to disclose are not grounds for annulment of the contract but the insurer can withdraw from the contract within three months from the day of the knowledge of the misrepresentation. If the accident occurs before the insurer has knowledge of the falsity or failure to disclose, or before the term for notification has expired, the amount due is reduced in proportion to the difference between the premium agreed upon and the premium which would have been paid if the true situation had been known (Article 1893 CC).

Chapter 11. Modification of Risk: Cessation, Reduction and Aggravation of Risk

154. The stipulation of the insurance contract requires that at all times the insurer should be made aware of the modification of the risk, which has a deep influence on the insurance contract.

The Italian legal system builds the matter of variation of risk within three general categories: cessation (or end) of risk, reduction of risk, aggravation of risk.

All these three situations represent a supervening change in circumstances that are able to distort or modify the general principles applied in contract law. Each modification of risk has different effects on the insurance contract.

§1. CESSATION OF RISK

155. The end of the insured risk is the 'extreme case' of modification of risk. The rule applied is very simple: if the risk ceases, the contract itself is subject to termination (Article 1896 CC).

Different effects relate to the time at which cessation of risk occurs. In fact, if the risk ceases to exist after the contract has been entered into, the insurer is entitled to premiums until he/she receives notice of the ending of the risk. If, on the other hand, the effects of the insurance contracts are yet to begin, the insurer is entitled only to reimbursement for expenses.

§2. REDUCTION OF RISK

156. The second variation that may affect the insured risk is reduction. This case does not seem to create any specific difficulty, as the risk of possible conflict of interest between the parties is significantly limited and, generally, the insurer does not have any minimum level below which he/she refuses the risk.

In any case, the discipline provided by the Civil Code is based on a simple succession of events: the insured has the burden to notify facts that determine a reduction of risk to ensure that the insurer will be able to decide whether to rescind the contract or to reduce the premium (Article 1897 CC).[92]

§3. AGGRAVATION OF RISK

157. The case of aggravation of risk is undoubtedly the most tricky to solve as in this case the possible conflicts of interest between insured and insurer is at its highest level. Attention must be focused on the following points.

---

92. See R. Sacco & G. De Nova, 'Il contratto', in *Trattato di Diritto Civile*, ed. Rodolfo Sacco (Turin, 1993).

I. The Discipline in Case of Aggravation of Risk: The Need for a Special Rule for Insurance Contracts

158.   The presence of a special rule for insurance contracts is a consequence of two main reasons. First, in insurance law it appears necessary to escape from the rule applied in general contract law, allowing for the termination of the contract in case of supervening circumstances (the limits and characteristics of this rule will not be discussed here, but let us consider the general principle of *rebus sic stantibus* set by Article 1467 CC).

Second, one should mention the necessity to escape from another principle of the law of contracts, in particular that of Article 1469 CC, according to which the rules of supervening hardship of the contracts are not applied to contracts that are aleatory by their nature (such as insurance) or for the intention of the parties.

II. Definition of Aggravation of Risk

159.   A possible definition of aggravation of risk can be inferred from Article 1898 CC: an increase of risk occurs when, had the insurer been aware of the fact, he/she would not have concluded the contract or would not have agreed on the same terms.

Nevertheless, it is generally accepted[93] that this cannot be a satisfactory definition, as we are dealing with a subjective notion of aggravation of risk. In other words, aggravation of risk does not correspond to an evaluation of probability that can be neutrally and objectively defined or observed, but the model is that of the insurer's perspective. This aspect, as we will see, has a direct effect on the definition of the insured's duty to notify.

In any case, the insurer has a duty to prove the relevance of the increase of risk on determining the insurance premium, according to the general principle of the proof of the fact that extinguishes or modifies a right.[94]

160.   As far as the dynamic approach towards aggravation of risk is concerned, it should be noted that the law in action shows a partial contrast between the approach to the problem proposed by legal scholars and the case law. Not only have the courts always established that aggravation of risk must be a *new* fact (which means a fact not described or foreseen at the time of the conclusion of the contract), but also that solely *permanent* facts can be considered as a relevant aggravation of risk.[95] The majority of the legal doctrine considers, on the contrary, that every modification of the risk is relevant.

---

93. See Buttaro, *Diminuzione del rischio e diminuzione del valore della cosa assicurata*, GCCC, 1955, III, 353.
94. See Castellano, *Le assicurazioni private*, G.S. Big (Torino 1970); Chindemi, *Il rischio assicurativo e le sue modificazioni*, De Ass 1994, 441; Donati, *Trattato del diritto delle assicurazioni private*, I, 1952; II 1954; III 1956; La Torre, *Scritti di diritto assicurativo* (Milan 1979); Roitman, *L'aggravamento del rischio nel contratto di assicurazione*, ASS 1973, I, 337.
95. See Art. 2697 CC, which sets the general provision on the *burden of proof*: a person who asserts a right in judicial proceeding must prove the facts on which the right is based. A person who asserts

161. It is generally accepted that circumstances that have to be considered a normal development of a situation existing at the time the insurance was concluded (e.g., fair wear-and-tear of machinery or vehicle) are not to be considered an aggravation of the risk. In the same way, the increase of value of the insured object does not represent aggravation of risk. Another important aspect to be highlighted is that the aggravation of risk is a different concept from a 'risk not considered by insurance' or another of risk 'excluded by insurance'. In fact, the notion of aggravation of risk is generally expressed in terms of a *quantitative variation* of the very risk that was taken into consideration at time of the conclusion of the insurance contract. Consequently, whether the different risk is less or more serious than the one considered under insurance terms is irrelevant.

162. In the same way, under the hypothesis of 'excluded risk', we have a qualitative variation. Wherever it occurs, we are in the field of the interpretation of the single contract and we cannot apply Article 1898 CC.[96]

In conclusion, we can say that according to the Italian legal system a fact that causes aggravation of risk relevant as to Article 1898 CC must be (a) following the conclusion of insurance; (b) not anticipated by the parties at the time the contract was concluded; (c) exogenous to the material evolution of the insured risk, as well as (d) lasting; and (e) material, that is to say relevant for the evaluation of the insurance premium.

163. Following this description of the general rule for aggravation of risk, it is important to notice that the discipline is quite different for life insurance.

In fact, Article 1898 CC is part of the general rules provided for all insurance contracts (Articles 1882–1903 CC) and *should* consequently be applied to life insurance; nonetheless, Article 1926 CC defines a specific case of aggravation of risk, i.e., the change of profession of the insured. Conditions and time of notification, as well as consequences of the aggravation, differ from the general rule set for Article 1898 CC.

Consequently, the majority of Italian legal scholars and the case law consider Article 1898 CC not applicable to life insurance.

III. Relevance of the Role of the Insured in Determining the Aggravation of Risk

164. The Italian legal system considers it absolutely irrelevant whether the aggravation of risk is endogenous or exogenous to the insured. In other words, it does not matter whether it is the action of the insured that worsens the risk or events

---

the invalidity of such facts, or claims that the right has been modified or extinguished, must prove the facts on which the defence is based.
96. App. Milano, 18 Jul. 1952, in *Assicurazioni*, 1954, II, 2; Cass. civ., 5 Jul. 1976, No. 2490, in Mass. Giust. Ital., 1976, col. 636; Cass. Civ., 18 Jan. 2000, No. 500).

and acts not related to his/her will[97] (but see below for the differences on the effect on the duty of notification).

It is worth mentioning, in any case, that this first (implicitly codified) rule is often strengthened by the contract terms. Especially in contracts offered to professionals (and not consumers), the contract terms provide a partially different rule that worsens the position of the insured. From a general point of view, this is not a legitimate solution as Article 1898 CC, like the majority of insurance rules of the Civil Code, is a relatively mandatory rule as it cannot be modified in disfavour of the insured (see Article 1932 CC). Nevertheless, contracts often establish that in case of 'fault' (or voluntary facts) of the insured giving place to aggravation of risk, the insurer is entitled to refuse the payment independently of a true evaluation of the level of aggravation of risk occurred.[98]

IV. Duty of Information by the Insured

165. The Italian legal rule is that the insured has a duty to inform the insurer of any aggravation of risk. Nevertheless, the insured may not know what can be considered a material change of risk as previously defined. The accomplishment of the duty to inform has a direct effect on the payment of the premium: if the insured does not fulfil his/her duty to inform, then the contract will continue to be valid on the side of insured obligation (payment premium). Otherwise, the insurer does not have to fulfil his/her obligation (grant damages).[99]

From this point of view, the duty of information has been considered by some doctrines not as an obligation (*dovere*) for the insured but only as a burden (*onere*), or basis, to keep the contract valid. In other words, should the insured fulfil his/her duty of information, then he/she still has the right to claim for damages; otherwise, he/she would lose his/her right.[100]

166. The application of a legal rule similar to the Italian one requires the insured to know exactly what elements have to be taken into consideration by the insurer in order to fix the premium. In fact, the insured can clearly understand the relevant facts taken into consideration in order to fix the premium only with reference to particular lines of insurance.[101] This problem is a mere consequence of the fact that, even at the time preceding the conclusion of the contract, the legal discipline (Articles 1892–1893 CC) gives rise to numerous doubts and conflicts, due to the fact that we do not know the facts and situations that have to be declared to the insurer.

---

97. Castellano, *supra.*
98. Salandra, *Dell'assicurazione*, Comm. SB, Bologna-Rome 1966, 245. The rule provided by the actual civil code is completely different from the previous one set by the *Codice di Commercio*. In fact, the old *Codice di Commercio* established that the insurer supported only the fortuitous aggravation of risk. From this perspective, another principle was considered prevalent, that is to say the duty of the insured not to increase the risk. This rule has been rejected by the actual legislator and we agree with this second solution.
99. See i.e., credit insurance contracts.
100. Tribunale Napoli, 16 Nov. 1987, D GIUR 1990, 193.
101. Salandra, *supra*, 247.

In other words, the problem of an acceptable definition of aggravation of risk is a consequence of the fact that no clear rules exist with reference to the limit of declaration of the risk in the pre-contractual phase.[102]

167. The first consequence is that, in the Italian legal system, aggravation of risk is considered from a subjective perspective, taking into consideration what the position of the insurer according to the risk is. The second consequence is that we cannot apply a rule similar to the French one, according to which the insured is obliged to declare the variation of facts as they were declared in the application form (questionnaire). A similar result may nonetheless be reached only by application of the so-called good-faith clause, in particular Article 1375 CC.

168. A possible solution would then be to look both at the questionnaire and at the elements taken into consideration by the insurer in order to determine the premium. No 'softening' of this rule, especially with reference to the French solution, is provided in favour of the insured. In particular, the Italian solution does not take into consideration the concrete effect of delay in notifying the aggravation of risk on the insurer (i.e., whether breach of duty to notify did or did not cause prejudice to the insurer).

V. Terms and Forms of Notification

169. The increase of risk may be voluntary or involuntary. As previously seen, the two cases are equally treated by the law with reference to the consequences on the insurance cover. On the other hand, the distinction has important effects on the duty of notification (which, according to Article 1898 CC, has to be given 'immediately'):

(a) for a voluntary increase of risk, the notification has to be given immediately and without any delay after the increase appears. In other words, the interpretation of 'immediate notice' is against the insured;
(b) if aggravation of risk depends on involuntary facts, the notification has to be given as soon as the insured knows of them.

The distinction between the two can be read in the light of Article 1375 CC that requires the parties to the contract to act in good faith.

170. The insured can perform his/her duty of information even orally. This freedom of legal form implies also that the proof of notification can be given in any way by the insured party.[103]

---

102. That is, for motor liability insurance.
103. In fact, in the silence of the legislators, the courts have attributed to the questionnaire (eventually given by the insurer) a sort of guide role, in the sense that it can operate to reverse the burden of proof of which facts are relevant or not to the insurer.

VI. Consequences of Aggravation of Risk

171. When considering the effects of aggravation of risk we have to think both of the effects on the contract and of the relation between the aggravation of risk and the incident occurring before the decision of the insurer to terminate (or the proposal to modify) the contract.

VII. Effects on the Contract

172. If the insurer can prove he/she would have assumed the risk for a different premium or would have not assumed the risk at all, he/she is entitled to terminate the contract. Only particular contract terms or a following proposal by the insurer may re-introduce the possibility of a modification of the premium in order to avoid the termination.

In particular:

(a) if the aggravation of risk is such that the insurer would not have assumed the risk, the insurer is allowed to notify termination of contract. The insurer must inform the insured within one month after the acknowledgement of the aggravation. The termination has immediate effect (if the insurer shows that he/she would not have insured the aggravated risk). In case of an accident, the insurer can refuse payment;

(b) if this is not the case, the insurer maintains the right to terminate the contract. Similarly, he/she has to notify the decision within one month from the acknowledgement of aggravation but, in this second case, the termination of contract (and of the cover) is set at fifteen days from the communication. If the incident occurs before the insurer elects to terminate (or to modify the contract), the insurer is entitled to reduce the payment.

In both cases, the insurer is entitled to the premiums for the period of the communication of the aggravation.

VIII. Relationship between the Aggravation of Risk and the Insured Event

173. The rule expressed in the Italian Civil Code does not require aggravation to play a direct or relevant role on the causation of the accident. This is a consequence of the subjective perspective, which means that the aggravation of risk is a matter affecting the evaluation of the insurer.

If an incident occurs, the payment can be refused or the entity of the payment reduced even if no relation exists between the aggravation of risk and the incident. The rule can be explained taking into consideration insurance techniques and especially the fact that every increase of risk has an effect on economic-risk management. Besides, the rule is an application of utmost good faith in order not to favour possible fraudulent attitudes of the insured who did not notify the increase of risk.

A minor part of the legal doctrine, however, has a different position considering that only an increase of risk connected to the verification of the accident should be taken into consideration in order to refuse or reduce the payment.[104]

---

104. Even by witnesses. See Salandra, 'Dell'assicurazione', in *Commentario diretto da Scialoja-Branca* (Bologna-Rome, 1966).

Chapter 12. The Insured Event: Procedure and Obligations of the Insured when the Insured Event Occurs

§1. GENERALITIES

174. Whenever an insured event occurs, the law establishes that some onus and duties should be carried out by the insured party. The first onus on the insured is to prove that he/she has sustained a loss within the terms of the policy.

175. Once the insured has established that the loss has been experienced, it is an onus on the insurer to try to demonstrate and prove that an exception or exclusion applies. This is a specific application of the general rule provided by Article 2697 CC.

176. With reference to the insured event, some duties are the summarized of the insured. The accomplishment of these duties – which can be preliminarily as responsibility to duty of notification and duty of salvage – is intended in the interest of the parties to the insurance contract but also in the interest of society as a whole, which can be damaged by the verification of a negative fact.

The relevant time, in order to determine when such duties arise, is the occurrence of the event as it is described (by law or) by contract. The exact definition of this time is necessary to distinguish the activities that represent a mitigation of the damage or loss (salvage) from those that prevent the occurrence of the insured event itself.

177. As previously announced, insurance contract law provides that two main duties are the responsibility of the insured if the insured event occurs: duty of notification and duty of salvage (Articles 1913–1914 CC). From a systematic point of view, these rules are specific provisions applicable to indemnity insurance (Articles 1904–1918).[105] Liability insurance is in a separate position. In fact, it is commonly accepted by the legal doctrine and the majority of case law that the duty of salvage is not applicable to liability insurance or, at least, it is not designed in the general terms (this second interpretation is the one the writer prefers).

In fact, it is quite obvious that, except for the case of fraud, the responsibility of the insured in causing the event and the consequent damage are the object of the insurance coverage itself. Consequently, the payment of the insured sum cannot be excluded only because of a negligent activity of the insured in the salvage phase. Besides, it has been pointed out that the activity of the insured may be relevant with reference to the mitigation of damages, e.g., when his/her activity can reduce the negative consequences of a tort action.

---

105. See in favour of the first solution: Donati, *Trattato di diritto delle assicurazioni private*, vol. I, 152 and following editions. Scalfi, 'Assicurazione (contratto di)', in *Digesto, disc. Comm.*, 1987, 355. Bocca, 'Aggravamento del rischio appreso dall'assiucratore in occasione del sinistro', in DPAssic., 1964, 119. In favour of the second solution Salandra, *supra*, 250.

178.   Particular problems also arise for the application of the duty of salvage with reference to personal-accident insurance. Nonetheless, in principle all these problems are sorted out by case law, as no exception to the application of the duty of salvage is present in the law.

In a very simple and preliminary intent, we can remember that Article 1913 CC establishes a duty to notify the occurrence of the insured event. The primary purpose of the notice of loss is obviously to allow the insurer to know immediately what has happened, to have a reasonable opportunity to protect his/her rights and to verify the circumstances of the loss (talking with witnesses, examining the records, preserving the physical evidence, etc.).

179.   As commonly known, these activities are essential to determine if a loss is covered by the contract or for the preparation of a defence in case of action by third parties in liability insurance. In other words, the provisions concerning acknowledgement requirements are intended both in the interest of the insured and in the interest of the insurer, and not for competition between them.

180.   Notwithstanding the importance of the notion, the legal system does not have a specific definition of insured event, nor does it seem that it would be necessary in order to reduce litigation. In fact, in some cases the contract itself introduces a specific definition of the insured event with all consequences of law at the time the duties of the insured begin and the determination of the amount of damages.

181.   No specific obligation arises by law on the insured according to special branches of insurance. In fact, Articles 1913 and 1914 CC apply to all indemnity insurances. Besides, the contract sometimes imposes such specific duties in very clear terms.

§2.   THE DUTY TO NOTIFY THE OCCURRENCE OF THE INSURED EVENT

I.   Duty to Notify

182.   The duty to notify the loss or, more in general, the occurrence of the insured event is primarily the responsibility of the insured. In any case, the loss notified by all other subjects is effective and valid.

In a contract on behalf of a third person (Article 1891 CC), the obligation is primarily the responsibility of the insured, even though the contractor in the position to know the occurrence of the insured event has a general duty to inform the insurer.

183.   The notification must be given to the insurer or the agent where the contract was signed.

184.   The notification can be given in any possible way: both written and oral communications are valid and effective. No specific form is required: the only relevant aspect is the knowledge by the insurer (this is an application of the general principle of freedom of forms).

II. Content of the Duty to Notify

185. No specific information is required by law, except for the notification of the event itself. Besides, the insurance contract often requires the inclusion of specific notions and information, given that the insured must immediately provide specific documents and papers documenting the event. Nonetheless, these further requirements (and the lack of them) cannot invalidate the accomplishment of the duty of notification but only affect the consequence of the misbehaviour of the insured in terms of reducing the indemnity if a prejudice is proved (see below).

A. *Terms*

186. The notification must be made within three days from the time the insured event occurs or from the time the insured party knows its occurrence (Article 1913 CC).

The term can be modified by the parties (it is not covered by Article 1932 CC, which stipulates the non-modification by the parties if not in favour of the insured).

A special term is provided only for the insurance on the mortality of the animals, where the notification has to be made within twenty-four hours.

187. As the notification is necessary in order to put the insurer in a condition to verify the circumstances of the loss, no notification is necessary if the insurer (or the authorized representative) has had other knowledge of the event or if, within the prescribed delay of three days, it takes an active part in the salvage.

188. As mentioned above, the initial term is the beginning (the first sign) of the insured event, if known by the insured.

If the insured event has a progressive formation (in example in credit insurance or liability insurance) the duty of notification and of salvage begins at the first signs that can be perceived, here including every fact that is relevant for the determination of the event.

B. *Proof of the Event*

189. No specific rules are provided for the proof of the insured event so that reference should be made to the general principles on the burden of proof provided in Book Six of the Civil Code.

In particular, according to Article 2697 CC, one party has to prove all the facts that provide a foundation to his/her right, while the other party has to prove the eventual existence of facts that modify, or exclude, the right (Article 2697 CC). For example, if the insured event occurs, the insured only has the duty to demonstrate that the fact happened and that that same fact corresponded to the notion of insured event.

On the other hand, if the insurer wants to refuse payment, he/she has the duty to prove the existence of a specific exclusion of coverage (i.e., the event is related to war risks, if these are excluded) or that he/she suffered a prejudice by non-compliance with the duty of salvage.

C. Duty to Notify and Cooperate in the Transfer of Information and Documents

190. The Italian system does not provide any specific rules with reference to the content of the duty of transfer of documents and information. In any case, the whole procedure in case of damage requires respect for the principle of good faith (if not *uberrima fides*) in the execution of the contract, so that the insured must make all the information he/she has which can be useful for the determination of the causes of the event.

III. Prevention and Mitigation of Damage

A. General Concepts

191. The insured has legal duty to do whatever is possible in order to avoid or mitigate the damage. This is the most general specification of the duty of salvage set by Article 1914 CC (*l'assicurato deve fare quanto gli è possibile per evitare o diminuire il danno*).

From a general point of view, it is important to clarify that no duty of salvage exists before the time at which the insured event occurs. In other words, the law does not set a duty to prevent the insured event, but only to avoid the negative consequences of the insured event itself or to mitigate those consequences.

The activity of the insured before the insured event occurs is, in fact, relevant under Article 1900 CC. Therefore, it will be evaluated according to principles of causation of the insured event (it will be recalled that Article 1900 CC establishes a lack of coverage in case of events caused by fraud or gross negligence of the insured – provided that, between the two, only gross negligence may eventually be covered by an express contract term).

The distinction is, in fact, quite important in order both to establish whether the duty of salvage was satisfied, and to determine whether the insurer has a duty to recover the insured for the fees occurred (see below).

192. Despite its importance, the distinction between action to prevent or mitigate damages and action to prevent the causation of the insured event is not always clear.

The need to distinguish between the two gives rise to a number of cases before the civil courts, especially in specific lines of insurance when the insured event has a progressive and repetitive nature (product liability is a clear example, with problems in distinguishing cases of recall of the product).

193. Two further aspects should be clarified. The first is the attempt of the courts to remove the time barrier between prevention of the event and prevention or mitigation of consequential damage. In fact, in very few cases, the courts have tried to bind the insurer to the payment of the damage for the insured things when it was the consequence of protection measures put in place by the insured. This is so even if, from a technical point of view, the measure was taken before the insured event occurred (the case was that of a car damaged by the fusion of the engine because of the manumission of the insured in order to prevent it from being stolen).[106] Besides, we should remember that this interpretation is not praised by the majority of legal doctrine.

In other cases the courts have established that no reduction of payment can be proposed by the insurer when specific measures of protection were required by contract. Therefore, if they are useless, the insurer cannot request the application of the rule of default of the insured and claim non-compliance with the duty of salvage (in this case it is important to distinguish whether the measure of protection is a condition for the insurance or a measure of salvage).

194. It should be pointed out that the law only requires the positive action of the insured in order to prevent or mitigate the loss, not a positive result of that action.

B. Expenses

195. The expenses sustained by the insured in order to prevent or mitigate the loss are a burden of the insurer even if their amount passes the maximum insured sum (Article 1914 CC). The rule is intended to mitigate the chance that the insured does not recoup the costs sustained for the prevention of the damage and, therefore, provide an incentive for the insured event.

In any case, the insurer is not compelled to reimburse the costs that relate to unreasonable costs (literally: *spese fatte inconsideratamente* – for example, if the insured destroys a very expensive car in order to pursue a thief for a very cheap item).

196. The insurer is also obliged to cover the insured for all material damages that are a direct consequence of the salvage (once again the limit to his/her duty is the proof that the costs were made unreasonably).

Whether the expense is reasonable or unreasonable is a matter of fact that has to be settled in accordance with good faith as required by Article 1176 CC. Besides, as the application of the principle of good faith is deeply related to the circumstances of the actual situation, a certain discretionary power is given to the judges and they often relate to the uses of the specific branch of insurance involved.

---

106. It will be recalled that the Italian legal system provides three sections of rules, the first applicable to all insurance contracts (Arts 1882–1903), the second to indemnity insurance (Arts 1904–1918 CC) and the third to life insurance (Arts 1919 et seq.).

On more occasions, legal doctrine has stressed the fact that the concrete evaluation should be done taking into account the particular condition of stress and emergency under which the insured acted.

In any case, the insurer can participate and play an active role in the salvage. Sometimes this is established even in the contract as a supplement any duty of the insurer. If the insurer participates in the salvage, he/she is obliged to anticipate the expenses if requested by the insured.

IV. Sanctions for Non-compliance with the Duty to Notify or Mitigate

197.   Article 1915 CC provides sanctions for non-compliance to the duty of notification or of salvage. In both cases, the insurer has a right to refuse the payment of the indemnity if the insured fraudulently does not inform the insurer of the damage or he/she does not accomplish the duty of salvage.

The existence of fraud does not require the specific intent to procure damage to the insurer, but only that the insurer was aware of the existence of the duty of salvage and of non-compliance.

If such duties are not accomplished, but without any fraudulent intent, the insurer only has a right to reduce the payment according to the prejudice he/she has suffered.

198.   The insurer has the burden to prove the existence of fraudulent intent or, in case of fault, the mere prejudice suffered.[107] The determination of the prejudice is a matter of fact.

Looking more closely to the concrete application of this principle of law, we can say that the insured is obliged to take an active role in order to mitigate and avoid damage, but the law does not require that his/her action achieve positive results.

---

107. Cass., 7 Sep. 1984, No. 4786, in *Foro it.*, 1985, I, 188.

Chapter 13. The Right of Subrogation

§1. GENERAL PRINCIPLES

I. Notion of Subrogation

199. In general terms, subrogation is the substitution of one person for another so that the person substituted is subrogated and succeeds to the rights of the other.

Article 1916 CC provides the right of subrogation of the insurer as a special case of subrogation.

200. The right of the insurer is a 'derivative one', which means that the third party can put forward to the insurer all possible objections and that in no case can the insurer's right be greater than the right transferred from the insured.

The fact that the insurer's right is not original but just repeats that of the transferor explains why the insured cannot prejudice the right of the insurer, sanctioning that he/she is obliged to relieve the insurer of any damage to the right of subrogation.

II. Aims of Subrogation in Insurance

201. The functioning of subrogation in insurance permits a number of results. The fundamental aim of the subrogation right of the insurer is to respect the indemnity principle, so that the insured who has been satisfied cannot recover the equivalent of the damage twice. In other words, subrogation facilitates an adjustment of rights in order to avoid unjust enrichment of the insured by substituting one person (the insurer) for the other (the insured) with regard to some claims or rights.

The insurer is consequently substituted with regard to all or a part of the rights that the insured has of receiving compensation from another party or source.

There is no doubt that the need to avoid a double recovery of the insured is to be read as a principle of public law. Consequently, subrogation is applicable in all forms of indemnity insurance.

202. Another positive result reached by subrogation is the reduction of the premium, as the insurer knows that according to subrogation he/she has the chance to recover part of the sum paid.

§2. EFFECTS AND FUNCTIONING OF SUBROGATION IN INSURANCE

I. Automatic or Voluntary Functioning of Subrogation

203. There is an urgent discussion about the time at which, according to Article 1916 CC, subrogation applies, and in particular whether it applies automatically or after a specific declaration by the parties after the insured event occurs.

In fact, if it is univocally assumed that subrogation does not arise until the insured has been indemnified for the particular event, it is under discussion whether the subrogation automatically takes place after the payment or if it derives from a declaration of the insurer who wants to exercise the right in question.

According to the first interpretation, the subrogation applies automatically after the payment because it is not up to the parties to determine whether the subrogation should have effect or not; this solution is motivated by the fact that the inactivity of the parties may give rise to a violation of the indemnity principle.

204. According to some other authors, the substitution of the insurer in the rights of the insured is not automatic but it should derive from a declaration of will by the insurer. An important effect of this interpretation would be that, if the insurer does not use its right of subrogation and consequently does not exercise this right, the insured might still be able to do it, if it is not the indemnity principle. This solution would avoid the unjust enrichment of the third liable party.[108] Both solutions are accepted by the case law.

II. Exception to Subrogation by Law or by Contract

205. There are cases where subrogation does not apply because of specific rules of law or because of some form of agreement between the parties.

206. With reference to exclusions by law, it should be remembered that Article 1916 CC provides that, except in case of fraud, subrogation does not take place when the damage is caused by children, affiliated children, ascendants or other persons related by blood or affinity to the insured and living permanently with him/her, or by domestic servants. The reason for this is quite clear as it is intended to avoid the rise of tension between family members and which might result in damage to the insured himself/herself who is close to the liable person.

In addition to exclusion by law, the insurer may forgo his/her right by express agreement in particular situations, provided that the right of subrogation does not result in the unjust enrichment of the insured.

III. Prejudice to the Right of Subrogation

207. The insured is liable to the insurer for the prejudice caused to his/her right of subrogation (Article 1916 CC). This solution derives from the fact that subrogation is a 'derivative' right so that the insurer receives what the insured gives him/her. This duty not to give prejudice to the right of subrogation is based on the law and more generally on the principle of the execution of contract duties in good faith.

---

108. Trib. Bolzano, 7 Nov. 1984, Ass., 1985, II, Mass. No. 65.

Chapter 14. Insurance on Behalf of a Third Party or for Whom it May Concern

§1. THE GENERAL RULE

I. Definition

208. Italian legislation provides specific rules for insurance on behalf of a third party and insurance for whom it may concern. The two cases are ruled by Article 1891 CC and they have in common the distriction between the identity of the contractor (*contraente* in Italian) and the insured (*assicurato*). In both cases, nevertheless, there is no representative activity because the contracting party acts in its own name and not in the name of another person (the case of a representative activity – or agency scheme – is instead considered by Article 1890 CC).

The difference between the two models regulated by Article 1891 CC is that in insurance on behalf of a third named party, the insured is exactly identified when the contract is agreed, while in insurance for whom it may concern, the name of the insured (or insured persons) is determined when the contract has already been made. The nature of the relationship between the contracting party and the insured one is irrelevant to the law.

209. In order to better understand the rules concerning contracts of insurance on behalf of a third party, from the point of view of the Italian legal system it is important to say that Article 1891 CC is a specific application to the insurance field of the general principles of Article 1411 CC regarding contracts in favour of a third party.

In fact, this expression (contract in favour of a third party) is applied both to the cases of Article 1891 CC and more in general for contracts with positive effects on a third party.

The last case will be left out of the analysis as it mainly refers to life insurance, which attributes the right to claim for indemnity in the case of death of the contractor to other persons called 'beneficiaries' (Article 1920 CC).

§2. INTEREST IN INSURANCE AND DISTRIBUTION OF RIGHTS AND DUTIES

I. Interest in the Contract

210. It needs to be specified that, according to the general rules of insurance law, the contracting party generally has all the rights and duties arising from the contract. Application of this rule might be inconsistent with the case of insurance on behalf of a third party, since the stipulation of the contract by the contractor would be in disagreement with Article 1904 CC, which requires a valid interest in the insurance deal. That is why the above-mentioned Article 1891 CC establishes a different rule implying that all the rights are to be given to the insured, while the contractor can exercise these rights only with the consent of the insured himself/herself. The rule allows no derogations.

211. A fundamental consequence is that the peculiar structure of the contract has to be declared at the time of the agreement, the risk being that of the invalidity of the contract as an application of the principle of lack of interest in the insurance.

212. From a practical point of view, the stipulation on behalf of a third party can result both from an express clause (using the words *per conto*, i.e., on behalf of) or by facts, i.e., by putting the name of the owner of the insured good in the insurance policy.

213. It should be pointed out that, since a quite general indication of the third party is sufficient to make the agreement valid (in the example, the reference to the name of the owner), a certain confusion may arise. In other words, it is often a matter of litigation whether the contracting party has intended to stipulate in his/her own interest (because, for example, he/she has a right to the good different from the right of property) or if he/she wanted to stipulate on behalf of a third party.

II. Payment of the Premium

214. As mentioned above, the obligations arising from the contract are borne by the contracting party, if they are not of a nature that can be solely performed by the insured. Let us consider an example. The contracting party has to pay the premium and has to collect the relevant document. However, the contractor has the right to collect both the premiums paid and the contract expenses from the insured; he/she also owns a *privilegio* (which can here be translated as a form of *lien*) over the amount due, and he/she will be satisfied with precedence over the other creditors of the insured.

No other obligation is provided by the law with reference to the payment of the premium, even though quite often the parties agree on a clause that compels the insurer to inform the insured in the case of non-payment so that he/she can substitute the contracting party in order to avoid lack of cover.

III. Duties of Declaration

215. While applying the principle mentioned above, most of the information duties generally have to be fulfilled by the insured, but in principle nothing excludes some information being provided by the contracting party. In this case, Article 1894 CC provides that if the insured has knowledge of non-disclosure or wrong declaration made by the contracting party, rules set by Articles 1892–1893 CC are applicable in favour of the insurer. It is important to remember that in the case of misrepresentation or fraudulent or gross negligence in disclosure, Article 1892 CC provides the rule that if the insurance concerns more than one person or thing the eventual invalidity of the contract does not affect the position of the others. These rules can be applied to insurance on behalf of a third party or for whom it may concern if the contract is made in the form of a group insurance (e.g., contracts made by the bank on behalf of the clients, or by employers on behalf of their employees).

IV. Disclosure and Information about Modification of Risks

216. It is well known that the duty of information is not completed contextually on the conclusion of the contract but goes according to the modification of risk during the contract itself. On this subject, the solution is non-univocal, also because the law does not expressly consider the case applied to insurance on behalf of a third party.

217. The first rule is, quite logically, that a party can inform the insurer only about the facts that the insured party knows. In the case under discussion, the contractor or the insured has to make the declaration of the relevant facts concerning their sphere of activity or knowledge, which generally corresponds to the set of declarations made at the time the contract was entered into.

Besides, we should also mention the general rule of utmost good faith. It binds both the insured and the contracting party to inform the insurer about changes to the relevant facts they know, even if, in a technical way, they refer to the position of the other subject and even if the other party made the initial declaration about it (modification of risk).

218. The consequences are in any case different from case to case. For example, in case of cessation of risk, the contracting party is the only one who has an interest in informing the insurer because he/she is otherwise obliged to go on with the payment of the premium, even though of course the declaration made by the insured is equally valid and relevant.

In case of aggravation of risk, it is mainly the insured that is affected by the non-declaration, so that he/she has a duty to declare every change of risk; execution according to the good faith principle, nevertheless, compels the contracting party to inform the insurer if he/she knows of the occurrence of a relevant fact.

V. Defences

219. Defences that can be raised under the contract against the contracting party can also be raised against the insured.

§3. Differences between Life and Non-life Insurance on Behalf of a Third Party

220. Article 1891 CC applies to both life and non-life insurance, since no specific provisions are given for any of them. Doctrine augments the function of Article 1891 through the interpretation of Article 1920 CC, at least partially; nonetheless, there is no complete coincidence between the beneficiary of the insurance described in Article 1920 and the third party implicated in the insurance.

On the other hand, the utility of a third-party life insurance model emerges from the identification of the contractor's interests to close the contract. For example, the contractor might carry an obligation to a third party and he/she might pay his/her due by making a contract on behalf of his/her creditor.

Furthermore, a difference between life insurance 'on behalf of' (Article 1891 CC) and 'in favour of' (Article 1920 CC) the third party lies in the fact that the first case allows the third party to claim the obligation while in the second case the contractor is free to change the beneficiary.

221. In order to summarize the distribution of rights and duties, we can say that the contractor has all the duties arising from the contract, such as the payment of the premiums and collection of documents, except for duties that can only be carried out by the insured, such as certain declarations on the risk, notice of the insured event, duty to save property.

222. The insured has the rights arising from the contracts, unless a different solution is agreed on by the parties.

223. The rules of Article 1891 CC apply both to life and non-life insurance. Marine insurance is included.

§4. CASE LAW

224. In some cases, the problem is to determine whether the contract is on behalf of a third party or not. The case law generally tends to consider the equivalence between the explicit indication of a third person in the contract under examination (i.e., the owner) and the inference of it. This results from other expressions of similar value or from the complex of contract clauses (i.e., a special annex to the contract regulating the specific rights of the insured-beneficiary or the solution of practical problems resulting from the trilateral structure of the contract).

§5. FINAL REMARKS

225. The Italian legal system lacks reference to the discipline of contracts on behalf of a third party or for whom it may concern. The only relevant rules are those of Articles 1891 and 1894 CC, so that the case law and legal doctrine have done much work to fill in the gaps of the legal sources. Nevertheless, the fact that the case law is not clear on a number of problems would be a significant element for the legislator in order to take action on the matter.

The importance of the contractual structure we are discussing is increasing more and more due to the activity of banks and other financial entities (financial institutions, employers, associations and clubs) to stipulate on behalf of third parties or for whom it may concern, and more in general in the light of the growth of group insurance agreements.

Chapter 15. Double Insurance or Insurance with more than One Insurer

226. Double insurance exists where more than one policy covers the same risk in the same subject matter. The matter is regulated under Article 1910 CC.

In such cases, which are defined as *assicurazione cumulativa* or *assicurazione presso diversi assicuratori*, a plurality of insurance contracts exists.

227. Judicial pronouncements have clarified that the following elements must exist in order for double or multiple insurance to exist: (a) the existence of the same object of the risk (i.e., the same house); (b) the same covered risk (i.e., fire); (c) the same duration and validity of the insurance (contemporary covers); (d) the same interest. This last element – the same interest – is fundamental and clarifies the fact that even if more than one policy covers the same risk, two or more insured persons could be entitled to receive different payments or benefits from two insurance covers, given the diversity of the interests.

228. If the presence of all such elements is confirmed, double insurance consequently exists, and the law requires the insurer to inform all the other insurers (Article 1910 CC).

229. The basic principle for the duty of notification is respect for the indemnity principle, so that the insured does not recover more than the damage suffered.

Chapter 16. Special Rules Concerning Indemnity Insurance

§1. THE INDEMNITY PRINCIPLE AND ITS APPLICATION

230. The indemnity principle is the basis of non-life insurance contracts. The relevance of the indemnity principle is reaffirmed by a number of specific provisions. In particular, Article 1904 CC provides that a contract of insurance against property damage is void if at the time when the insurance is to begin, the insured has no interest in the property for which he/she may be compensated in case of damage.

231. Another application of the indemnity principle is that the insurer is bound to compensate the insured for the damage resulting from the accident in a manner and to the extent stipulated in the contract. The insurer is liable for anticipated profits only if he/she had expressly undertaken such obligation (Article 1905 CC).

232. Finally, Article 1906 CC provides that if the defect has increased the damage, the insurer, unless otherwise agreed, is liable for the damages only to the extent that he/she would have been liable if the defect had not existed.

§2. ALIENATION OF THE INSURED PROPERTY

233. A transfer of the insured property is not cause for the termination of the insurance contract. An insured who fails to notify the insurer of the transfer or to notify the acquiring party of the existence of the insurance contract remains liable for the payment of the premiums maturing after the date of transfer (Article 1918 CC).

§3. PARTIAL INSURANCE (OR UNDERINSURANCE)

234. If the insurance covers only a part of the value of the insured property at the time of the accident, the insurer is liable for the damages in proportion to such part, unless otherwise agreed (Article 1907 CC). The ignorance of the insured of the underinsurance is irrelevant for the reduction of indemnity.

This limitation does not apply in the case of *polizze a primo rischio*.

Chapter 17. Limitation Period

§1. Ordinary and Short-term Limitation Period in Private Law

I. Ordinary Limitation Period

235. The fact that the limitation period is a key point of law and represents the intrinsic complexity of the system, which tends to balance the need to maintain in life a certain right of one party for the longest period possible and the need for certainty about facts, is witnessed by the large amount of litigation on the matter that also represents a major cause of professional liability for lawyers. A common definition of limitation period is that of a cause of extinction of a right for the passing of time.[109]

236. The rules concerning the limitation period are provided by Book VI (protection of rights) of the Civil Code.

The general rule is set by Article 2934 CC according to which all rights are extinguished by the prescription when the owner fails to exercise them within the time fixed by law. The ordinary limitation period (*prescrizione ordinaria*) here provided is ten years. This term applies unless derogated by other rules of law (all these cases are resumed as *prescrizioni brevi* – short-term limitation periods).

237. The most important derogation concerns the matter of tort liability and the rights of compensation for damages, where the term provided is five years;[110] damages resulting from circulation of vehicles of any kind are submitted to the limitation period of two years.

II. Limitation Period in Insurance

238. Among short-term limitation periods, one of the shortest is provided for insurance. In fact, Article 2952 CC provides that the limitation period in insurance matters is two years.[111]

It needs to be clear that this term refers both:

(a) to the right of the insurer to act for the payment of the premiums; and
(b) to all other rights arising from the insurance contract.

239. Before showing in depth the practical application of this short limitation period, it seems important to point out two facts.

The first one is that even if two years seem a short period, until 2008 the time limit was of one only year! In 2008, the Law 27 October 2008 no.166 has double

---

109. Donati, Volpe & Putzolu, *Manuale di diritto delle assicurazioni*, 163.
110. Vivante, *La prescrizione in materia di assicurazioni, Trattato di dirittto commerciale* (Milan, 1935); Scalfi, *I contratti di assicurazione. L'assicurazione danni* (Turin, 1991).
111. See Bussani & Venchiarutti, 'Tort Law', in *Introduction to Italian Law*, Lena & Mattei (eds), 234.

the prescription term; the law was approved under pressure of the consumer association with reference to the prescription rights in the so-called case of 'sleeping contracts': in fact, there were (and there still is) a large number of life insurance contracts which are not known by the beneficiaries, so that they lose their money for the running of the prescription time. In 2008, the problem was considered to be urgent to let the prescription time to one year, so it was modified for all insurance contracts.

240. In any case, when the one-year term applied, a question of constitutionality was raised with reference to the compatibility of such a short-term (one year) and a possible contrast with the principle of equality and rationality of the law set by Article 3 of the Italian Constitution.

In other words, the legal rule (Article 2952 CC) was attacked on the grounds of the real possibility for an insured to act and consequently obtain justice in case of fixation of such a short period, and even more in light of the importance of the insurance contract, where no technical reasons seem to support such a derogation to the ordinary prescription of ten years or at least to a longer one.

241. The Italian Constitutional Court has firmly rejected such an interpretation and has considered the rule set by Article 2952 CC to be perfectly congruent with constitutional rights. One could doubt that even a two years period is long enough, at least with reference to some kind of insurance policies and situations [112]

242. This clarified, we need to specify that the limitation period of one year applies only to insurance contracts (the limit of the notion is set by Article 1882 CC) and not to all other contracts – named or unnamed – offered by the insurers (i.e., guaranty contracts, capitalization, etc.).

III. Special Rules for Some Lines of Insurance or Rules Applying in Particular Situations

243. After specifying that the term of one year is the 'general period' for insurance law, some exceptions or simply some adjustments are applicable with reference to some lines of insurance or specific situations.

244. The most important ones are listed below.

A. *Limitation Period for Liability Insurance*

245. Liability insurance is submitted to the limitation period of one year but the prescription term runs from the day on which the injured person requests

---

112. Azzariti & Scarpello, 'Della prescrizione e della decadenza', in *Commentario al codice civile* a cura di Scialoja e Branca, sub Art. 2952, (Bologna-Rome, 1964).

compensation from the insured or files a claim against him/her (Article 2952 CC, paragraph 3).

Notice to the insurer of the request from the injured third person or of the action against him/her suspends the course of the prescription until the claim of the injured person is liquidated and made collectible, or until the right of the injured person expires.

This provision also applies to the action of the reinsured against the re-insurer for the payment of the indemnity.

B. Limitation Period in Reinsurance

246. The rights arising from the contract of reinsurance follow the limitation period of two years (Article 2952 CC, II).

C. Limitation Period for Motor Insurance

247. A special rule is provided for motor liability insurance with reference to the action of the third party against the insurer of the liable insured. In fact, Article 26 of Law No. 990/1969 (new rule 290 CAP) provides that the direct action of the third party against the insurer be submitted to the same limitation period of the action against the liable party. This is not, in fact, a true derogation to Article 2952 CC as it applies to the insurer–insured relation, but Article 26 plays an important role in the determination of the duty of the insurer.

Besides, if the third party acts only against the insured, the action of the insured against his/her insurer is submitted to the 'general' term of one year.

D. Limitation Period for the Action of the Insurer against Liable Third Parties

248. The action of the insurer is submitted to the same limitation period applicable to actions from the insured against third parties responsible for the damage. The action for the prejudice caused by the insured to the insurer's right of subrogation is one year; this right arises, in fact, from the insurance contract.

E. Some Social and Mutual Insurance

249. In some cases, the laws concerning mutual and social insurance provide for special rules with reference to limitation period. If not derogated, the general rule of one year is applicable.

§2. EFFECTS OF THE COURT JUDGMENT

250. According to the general rule, the judgment transforms the original limitation period into the ordinary one (ten years). In other words, each right for which the law provides a time limit shorter than ten years is prescribed on the lapse of ten years when a final judgment has been rendered with respect to that right (Article 2953 CC). The same rule applies to a ritual arbitration judgment. Some problems arise with reference to contract arbitration clauses and the consequent effects (see below, last paragraph on litigation).

§3. STARTING POINT OF THE LIMITATION PERIOD

251. The general rule is that prescription runs from the day when the right can be enforced (Article 2935 CC).

The rule is interpreted so that only juridical obstacles are relevant, while every other impediment in fact is irrelevant and does not interrupt or avoid the course of the prescription.

252. The tentative approach to limiting the extent of this principle and to giving relevance to subjective reasons to suspend the course of prescription have been refused by decisions of the Supreme Court.[113] The same result is accepted by the Supreme Court even in respect of a third beneficiary party which was not aware of the existence of the contract,[114] notwithstanding the position of the scholars who would overturn the limit with reference to the general clause of good faith.

253. According to this general rule, the period of limitation for the payment of the premium runs from the date of expiry of each instalment (Article 2952 CC). In all other cases, the prescription runs from the date when the right can be exercised. In most cases, the date is the same as when the accident occurs.

The delay is provided by law and cannot be modified by the parties either directly or indirectly.

§4. EXPIRY OF THE LIMITATION PERIOD

254. Some corollary rules clarify the practical way to determine the expiry and computation of the prescription. The first provides that, in all cases contemplated by the civil code and by other laws, the prescription incurs an expiry of the last day of the time limit of the prescription. The second deals with the computation of the time limits, as provided by Article 2963 CC and it provides that the term be calculated not taking into account the day on which the right can be exercised.

---

113. Corte Costituzionale 3 Dec. 1987 No. 458.
114. Cass. 28 Oct. 1994 No. 8909 GC 1995, I, 1292; Cass. 7 Sep. 1994 No. 7688.

§5. INTERRUPTION AND SUSPENSION OF THE LIMITATION PERIOD

I. Interruption of the Running of the Limitation Period

255. The time limit is interrupted in a number of cases provided by the law (Articles 2943 and 2944 CC). In particular, the prescription is interrupted by service of the paper by which judicial proceedings are commenced, both on the merit and for conservation or enforcement (Article 2943 I al. CC). The limitation period is also interrupted by actions in the course of judicial proceedings. In this case, the interruption is effective even if the court where the action is submitted lacks jurisdiction.

Prescription is also interrupted by any other acts able to place the debtor in default (Article 1219 CC) and by a duly served document whereby a party, in the presence of an agreement to arbitrate or an arbitration clause, declares to the other party the intention to start arbitration proceedings, hands in its claim and proceeds, on its own behalf, with the appointment of arbitrators (Article 2943 CC, III al.). In addition, the limitation period is interrupted by acknowledgement of right by the person against whom the right can be enforced.

256. The effect of the interruption of the limitation period is quite clear and well known: a new prescription begins as a result of the interruption (Article 2945 CC).

Besides, special rules apply under specific situations or positions of the parties involved.

In particular, if the interruption occurs because of one of the acts indicated in the first two paragraphs of Article 2943 CC, e.g., in case of judgment, the prescription does not begin until the judgment in the action becomes final.

In case of arbitration, prescription does not run from the time when the document containing the request for arbitration is served; it begins from when the award settling the dispute is no longer subject to appeal or the decision rendered on the appeal becomes res judicata.

II. Suspension of the Running of the Limitation Period

257. The limitation period is suspended according to the general rules of law. In general, the reason for the suspension relates to particular relations between the parties involved.

For example, as mentioned above, in liability insurance the notice to the insurer about the request of the injured third person or about the action instituted by him/ her suspends the course of the prescription until the claim of the injured person is liquidated and made collectible or until the right of the injured person is prescribed (Article 2952, 4 CC).

In addition, prescription is suspended on the grounds of a special relation between people (i.e., between married people, between the company and its representatives, and so on – Article 2941 CC) or for reasons of the condition of the owner of the right (i.e., minors, persons in war, etc. – Article 2942 CC).

§6. CONTRACTUAL ADAPTATION OF THE STATUTORY RULES GOVERNING LIMITATION PERIODS

258. No contractual modification of the statutory rules concerning a limitation period (in its terms or application) is allowed, or with reference to suspension, interruption or any other aspects concerning the limitation period. In fact, any agreement intended to modify the legal regulation of prescription is void. The courts give a very wide application to this rule.

259. One should remember, in any case, that the parties are free to set a specific period of *decadenza*. In other terms, the parties can agree on special clauses that have the effect of barring the action if a certain activity is done/not done or executed/not executed in a certain way or within a certain time (so-called forfeiture clauses).

The difference between prescription and such lapsing clauses is in fact very 'subtle' in terms of protection of the party. In all cases, the action is barred. That is why the law provides that stipulations establishing forfeiture clauses upon the expiry of the time limits are void. The same rule applies when such clauses make the exercise of the rights excessively difficult for one of the parties (Article 2965 CC).

§7. LITIGATION CONCERNING THE LIMITATION PERIOD

260. The limitation period has given rise to a number of cases concerning both general contract law and insurance contracts in particular. In most cases, the matter of litigation concerns the fixing of the starting point of the limitation period. In some others, it is the connection between the actions of third parties and the actions against the insurer that are of concern.

Some problems also arise with reference to the limitation period in accident insurance, especially with reference to the aggravation of personal injuries resulting from the accident and the terms on which the action has been brought to court.

261. Many problems arise with reference to arbitration clauses. The legal doctrine mostly seems to make a clear distinction between clauses that provide for a technical evaluation and clauses that introduce a true arbitration judgment. In the first case, the one-year prescription remains valid. In the second, the long limitation period applies.

The case law does not completely adhere to this view. In fact, most of the courts seem to consider the result of arbitration procedures coming from the contract as insufficient to transform the short limitation period into the ordinary one.

However, the contract clause that provides for the formation of the arbitration board and the consequent request of the insured to establish that board or the nomination of the expert and the consequent notice to the insurer (even if it does not suspend the limitation period) is nonetheless valid for the interruption. This is an application of the general principle that considers it an act showing the clear intention of the insured to exercise his/her right.

262. No legislation reform is under discussion. In fact, the original project for a Code of Private Insurances provided a section for the revision of the insurance contract law included in the Civil Code. This part of the project has been omitted in the final text.

Chapter 18. Mandatory Rules for all Insurance Contracts

263. Article 1932 of the Civil Code provides the mandatory character of a number of rules concerning the regulation of the insurance contract.

The aim of the rule is to improve the previous system of the Commercial Code where the majority of the rules were default rules and could be completely derogated by the parties.

Article 1932 CC has a double function: on the one hand, it provides for the inability to derogate for the provision if not in favour of the insured. The consequence of the violation of this rule is the invalidity of the derogation. This is considered the *pars destruens* of the rule. In addition, the invalid provision is substituted by law by the legal rule applicable to the case (Article 1932 CC, II al.). This is the *pars costruens* that allows the contract to have the necessary rule.

264. The mechanism provided by Article 1932 CC is a special application of Article 1339 CC concerning the invalidity of all contract clauses, and the general principles elaborated by the case law with reference to this article can be applied to Article 1932 too. In particular, the error or mis-knowledge of the party is not relevant.[115]

---

115. Cass. 18 Jun. 1998 No. 6062. Contra a minor part of the courts decisions such as Court of Appeal of Rome, 25 Nov. 1992, in DT, 1994, 217 with comment by Smirolo.

Part III. Property and Liability Insurance

Chapter 1. General Rules Applicable to Liability Insurance

§1. GENERAL CHARACTERISTICS OF THE COVERAGE AND DEFINITION

265. Liability insurance covers the insured's interest to be indemnified for the sums he/she is obliged to pay for liability towards third parties. The limits and extents of the liability covered are identified in the single insurance contract.

The first comma of Article 1917 CC defines the liability insurance contract:

> In liability insurance the insurer is obliged to indemnify the insured for damages which he is obliged to pay because of the events occurred during the insured period and resulting in the liability covered by the insurance contract. Damages deriving from fraudulent acts are excluded' (Article 1917, CC, I comma).

266. Liability insurance is to be considered part of insurance against damages.[116] This clarification is not merely theoretical as it indicates that the rules provided by the Civil Code for non-life contracts are applicable to liability insurance.

267. The risk covered by each single contract is strictly connected with the legal bases of the liability in question. In fact, policies distributed in the Italian market generally provide that the insured is covered in respect of sums he/she is legally liable to pay, without mention of the source of that liability (that could be qualified as liability in tort as well as contractual liability).

A liability insurance contract does not cover risks that the insured has voluntarily assumed towards third parties.

In addition, the limits of the covered risk relate to the insured person(s) as identified in the contract and to the kind of activities performed by the insured.

Further limits are set in the policies with reference to the types of damage recoverable. The coverage in generally limited to physical damages or damage to property, with exclusions of pure economic losses or damages for interruption of activity.

---

116. M. Rossetti, 'Commento Art. 1932 c.c.', in *Le assicurazioni. L'assicurazione nei codici. Le assicurazioni obbligatorie*, ed. La Torre (Milan, 389).

§2. ABSENCE OF A DIRECT ACTION OF THE VICTIM TOWARDS THE INSURER OF
THE LIABLE PARTY

268. In the Italian legal system, damaged third parties are not allowed to act
directly against the insurer of the liable party. This solution is inferred by the interpretation of Article 1917, II comma CC.

In fact, Article 1917 CC stipulates that the insurer has the possibility to pay the
due sum to the victim but he/she is obliged to do it only if expressly required by the
insured.

On the other hand, the victim does not have any right to act directly towards the
insurer, even if a lien (*privilegio*) in favour of the victim exists on the insured sum,
according to the provisions of Article 2767 CC. Case law allows the victim to exercise a surrogate action in case of inactivity of the insured.

269. The absence of the victim's right to act against the insurer of the liable
party is traditionally motivated with reference to the diversity of duties deriving
from the liability relation, on one side, and from the insurance contract, on the other
side.

The absence of a direct action of the victim against the insurer of the liable party
has been strongly criticized by legal doctrine suggesting that a more coherent protection of third parties not only requires such action but would also be in line with
the solutions applied in other European countries.[117] In fact, there is no doubt that
liability insurers generally negotiate directly on the insured's behalf with the victim
and pay the due sum into his/her hands. This demonstrates the existence of a direct
link between the victim and the insurer since the starting phase of the claim, which
may be relevant in order to support the possibility of a direct action.

The Italian courts have nevertheless consistently refused such a rule by virtue of
a literal interpretation of Article 1917 CC.

§3. THE DUTY TO PAY THE COSTS OF THE DEFENCE AND THE EVENTUAL RIGHT
OF THE INSURER TO ASSUME THE DEFENCE

270. Once he/she assumes by contract the duty to indemnify the insured if
he/she incurs liability, the insurer is also legally obliged to pay costs sustained by
the insured for the defence against the action brought about by third party within
the limit of one-quarter of the insured sum (Article 1917 CC, III comma). This is
considered an application of the more general duty to pay costs of salvage as set by
Article 1914 CC.

In any case, if the sum due to the victim exceeds the insured sum, the costs of
proceedings are divided between the insurer and the insured in proportion to their
respective interest.

---

117. Cass., 3 Mar. 1989, No. 1196; for a comprehensive analysis see Angeloni, *Assicurazione della
responsabilità civile* (Milan, 1958); A.D. Candian, *Responsabilità civile e assicurazione* (Milan,
1993); Franzoni, 'Responsabilità civile (assicurazione della)' in *Digesto, Disc. Comm.* (Turin,
1996), XII, 396.

271. Insurance contracts often provide for an additional agreement called *patto di gestione della lite*. This agreement is collateral to the legal duty to pay the costs of the defence and confers on the insurer the right to assume the defence of the insured in civil proceedings.

If the insurer exercises this right and consequently assumes the insured's defence, he/she has a duty to act properly. In other words, an insurer undertaking the defence of the insured must perform with due care and he/she is responsible towards the insured for damages.[118]

The obligation assumed by the insurer is qualified as an obligation of means (in opposition to obligations of results). He/she is consequently responsible under the specific hypothesis of *mala gestio*, i.e., eventual negligent activity of the insurer, if the insurer is obliged to pay damages to the insured.

272. With the exception of motor liability insurance (Law No. 990/1969, new rules Title X *Codice delle assicurazioni Private* CAP) and a few other forms of compulsory insurance, in all other cases the duty of the insurer to pay finds its source in the contract. The insurer consequently incurs a contractual liability in case of failure which determines damages to the insured in terms of prejudice to his/her reputation or if the sum finally due to the victim exceeds the maximum insured sum.

Damage flowing from the breach of the duty of care and *mala gestio* may include the entire amount of any excess judgment against the insured.

273. The case has often been considered in courts. In example, the insurer's liability for *mala gestio* has been declared where a possible transaction proposed by the victim has been unreasonably refused by the insurer.[119] The evaluation of such a refusal to pay or to make a transaction is made with reference to the advantage of the received proposal and its reasonableness.

Other cases of *mala gestio* relate to a situation where non-existing exceptions were imposed by the insurer or in case of vexatious action.[120]

§4. COMPULSORY LIABILITY INSURANCE

274. A person exposed to a certain risk is sometimes obliged to stipulate an insurance contract. This duty represents an important derogation to the principle of freedom of contract set by Article 1322 CC.

In some cases, the person obliged to enter the insurance contract is the victim himself/herself of a certain activity or potential damage situation, such as in case of compulsory insurance for personal accidents. This is called first party insurance.

---

118. See *inter alia* and for a precise description of the different positions of scholars A.D. Candian, *Responsabilità civile e assicurazione* (Milan, 1993).
119. A. Monti, *Buona fede e assicurazione* (Milan, 2001).
120. Cass. 27 Sep. 1999 No. 10696.

275. In other cases the person to take the insurance is the potentially liable party. In this case we talk about compulsory liability insurance or compulsory third-party insurance.

Compulsory liability insurance has the aim of protecting the victim of a tort from the eventual insolvency of the liable party, and protecting the liable party against losses to his/her patrimony.

276. In Italy, the number of instances of compulsory liability insurance provided by the law is increasing more and more, even though it is still low compared to those existing in foreign states.

In most cases, the introduction of a new hypothesis of compulsory liability insurance also sets the essential contents of the policy in order to determine the minimum standard and extent of the coverage.

277. As already mentioned, a peculiar aspect of the Italian discipline is the absence of a general direct action of the victim towards the insurer of the liable party. It is important to clarify that this rule applies even in cases of compulsory insurance if not otherwise provided by the law (i.e., the case for motor insurance). As a consequence, in most cases the victim can only act against the liable party who has in his/her turn the onus to call the insurer.

278. The most common forms of compulsory liability insurance relate to the exercise of transport activities, dangerous activities (oil and gas transfer, nuclear activities, etc.), public employment and activities (hospitals, vaccines, transfusions, etc.), maritime risks, or even the exercise of particular professions (fiscal consultants, insurance agents and brokers of insurance, no-profit organizations, tour operators, etc.).

The duty to be insured can derive from international, national or even regional laws.[121]

---

121. Cass. 10 Aug. 1982 No. 4474 AC, 1983, 284.

Chapter 2. Motor Vehicle Insurance

§1. LEGAL SOURCES OF LIABILITY FOR MOTOR ACCIDENTS

279. For a better understanding of the Italian system of motor liability insurance, it is useful to examine the existing liability system overall.

One of the most significant developments of the twentieth century was the widespread use of motor vehicles. Because drivers so frequently crash with third parties, vehicles and property, the traditional method of compensating motor accident victims based on tort liability was soon considered unfit for this kind of risk. It was quite evident that the effective protection of victims of road accidents required the introduction of a strict liability rule.

280. This is why Article 2054 CC – in derogation to the general rule of tort liability based on fault (Article 2043 CC) – establishes a joint and strict liability between the owner of the car and the driver for any damage caused by the circulation of vehicles. In particular, Article 2054 CC stipulates that the driver is liable for the damage caused to persons or to property by operation of the vehicle unless he/she proves that he/she did all that was possible in order to avoid the damage.

In the case of collision of vehicles it is presumed without proof to the contrary that each operator contributed equally to the damage. The owner of the vehicle (or in his/her place where existing the life tenant) is jointly liable with the driver unless he/she proves that it was driven against his/her will.

§2. COMPULSORY INSURANCE FOR MOTOR VEHICLES: AN OVERVIEW OF THE HARMONIZATION OF LAW IN THE EU MARKET AND OF LAW NO. 990 OF 24 DECEMBER 1969 (NEW RULE TITLE X OF CODICE DELLE ASSICURAZIONI PRIVATE)

281. The introduction of a system of strict liability for road accidents based on Article 2054 CC was unable to work properly without an adequate 'twin system' of compulsory insurance.

Compulsory insurance for all motor vehicles circulating on public roads was consequently introduced by Law No. 990 dated 24 December 1969. Since then, much water passed under the bridge. In particular, the creation of single European market for insurance and the need to facilitate free circulation and movements of persons has determined a strong harmonization of laws in the matter, so that a detailed description of the existing system of compulsory insurance for motor accidents may appear redundant for most readers.

Nonetheless, the general features of the existing laws as resulting after the implementation of the four generations of European motor directives are briefly explored in this chapter in order to better understand the specific problems faced by the Italian market at present.

282. The internal and European rules concerning motor insurance were united in Law No. 990 dated 24 December 1969, in DPR dated 24 November No. 973 and

in Law No. 57 dated 2001. These regulations have now been included and coordinated in Title X of the *Codice delle Assicurazioni Private*, from Articles 122–160
and Title XII, from Articles 170–172).

§3. THE DUTY TO BE INSURED

283. Article 1 of the Law No. 990/1969 (new rule Article 122 CAP) states the
duty to insure every vehicle circulating on the public roads or on private roads open
to public circulation.

The duty to stipulate the insurance contract is the responsibility of the owner of
the vehicle, the life tenant and more generally everyone who puts the vehicle into
circulation and makes use of it. The accomplishment of the duty to be insured has
to be proved by a certificate (*certificato di assicurazione*) which has to be permanently displayed on the top of the vehicle.

§4. THE DUTY TO INSURE AS THE RESPONSIBILITY OF INSURANCE COMPANIES: ITS CONTENT AND ITS VIOLATION

284. The Italian legal system is quite peculiar as it establishes a bilateral duty
for the insurance contract. In fact, while Article 1 of Law 990/1969 (new rule Article
122) affirms the duty to be insured, Article 11 of the same law (new rule Article 132
CAP) provides that insurance companies operating in Italy are obliged to accept all
insurance proposals that they may receive from potential insured persons.

The consequence of a failure to comply with the obligation to insure is a breach
of statutory provisions and attracts heavy pecuniary sanctions.

ISVAP has the power to supervise insurers in respect of the duty to insure and
can inflict sanctions on insurance companies for non-compliance with this duty.

285. In addition to the duty to accept insurance proposals coming from prospective insureds, insurance companies operating in Italy are obliged to establish in
advance all premiums applicable to motor insurance and to make them public at
each point of sale and even via the Internet.

This provision, which has been recently introduced after much parliamentary discussion, has the aim of putting the insured in a position to know in advance the premiums offered by each insurance company and at the same time to favour
competition between insurance companies acting in the Italian market.

286. It is well known, in any case, that the problem of transparency and the constant rise of motor insurance premiums is a very serious one in Italy and seems to
bear no similar proportion to that in other European states.

A significant proof of the dramatic increase in insurance premium rates – which
only in the year 2004 rose less than the inflation rate – was the decision adopted by
the Italian government, first with a Law Decree soon ratified by Law of the Parliament in 2000, to impose a block on rises in premiums for one year. The effect of

such a provision was the impossibility, for all insurance companies, of revising their rates notwithstanding any technical need to do that.

This decision was sanctioned by the European Court of Justice because it appeared to be in violation of the freedom to establish by law insurance premiums introduced by the third directive.

287. In fact, it should be remembered that the aim of the third Non-Life Directive (Directive EC/92/49) was to complete the internal market from the point of view both of the right of establishment and of the freedom to provide services. An essential element of this strategy was the principle of freedom to set premiums, so that the national authorities were from that moment on prevented from arbitrarily determining motor insurance premiums.

The European requirements had been duly implemented by the Italian legislation: in fact the Legislative Decree No. 175/1995 transposing the third Non-Life Directive (now *Codice delle Assicurazioni Private*) liberalized the rates for compulsory motor vehicle insurance (which had until then been subject to a price-control system, as in most European countries). As a consequence, the so-called CIP references (i.e., to say *classi interministeriali di premio* as the premium rates determined by the Ministry were called) disappeared and gave way to free market determination. A table of reference between the 'ex-CIP classes' and the new ones to be established by each company was introduced in order to allow the correct application of the *bonus-malus* system during the transitional period.

288. Nonetheless, in order to meet the following rise in premiums (some statistics report an increase up to 400% from 1995 to 1999), in 2000 Italy adopted a Decree 'containing urgent provisions to limit inflationary pressures' concerning various sectors, including compulsory motor vehicle insurance.

The aim of the legislator was to limit inflation, and this was to be countered by freezing compulsory motor vehicle insurance premiums. It is important to clarify that the rule had to be applied to all insurance undertakings, whether they had their registered office in Italy or carried on business there through branch offices or under the freedom to provide services. This was of course a symptom of non-discrimination between national and foreign companies!

Following the protest of a number of national and foreign insurers operating in Italy under the freedom of establishment or freedom to provide services, the problem was finally taken to the European institutions.

289. It was then up to the European Commission to finally accept the protest on the conviction that the approved Italian provisions infringed the principle of freedom to set premiums and the system for exchanging information provided for by the directive. Consequently the European Commission brought an action against the Italian Republic before the Court of Justice. Although the rate freeze is no longer in force, the Commission has expressly continued with its action which came to an end quite recently.

According to the court, Directive EC/92/49 was intended to secure the principle of freedom to set premiums in the field of compulsory motor vehicle insurance. This system implies the prohibition of any prior notification or approval of premium rates except within the framework of a general price-control system.

290. Consequently, the court has considered that the rules governing premium rates laid down in Italian legislation significantly restricted the freedom of insurance undertakings, including those operating under the right of establishment or the freedom to provide services, to set their premiums.

The Court then decided that the Italian legislation led to a selective intervention in the sector of compulsory motor vehicle insurance, without any direct link to the various measures in other sectors referred to by the Italian government, and held that this intrusion could not be justified on the ground that it formed part of a general price-control system. However, the court rejected the Commission's application with regard to the obligation imposed on insurance undertakings to communicate to a data bank the claims made against them.

It notes that the directive provides for the exchange of essential data between national authorities in order to prevent unjustified obstacles to the exercise of the right of establishment or the freedom to provide services; the information gathering provided for under the Italian legislation pursues a different anti-fraud objective from that pursued by the directive. Since the two mechanisms did not pursue the same objective, the Court considered that the one need not be regarded as incompatible with the other.

291. By virtue of the said decision of the Court of Justice and thanks to the natural expiry of the effects of the unlawful block of premiums, only control over the attitude of the insurance company with reference to (a) refusal to insure or (b) the (direct or indirect) evasion of the duty to insure is possible.

ISVAP is consequently allowed to determine if the insurance company has artificially abstracted from the basic elements necessary to determine the premium level in order to evade the duty to insure certain classes of risks.

Nonetheless, the fair market level can just be considered as an indication of a possible evasion which has nevertheless to be determined with reference to other elements.

292. The sanctions provided for the case of evasion of the duty to insure are very high. They are applicable both to Italian companies and to companies operating under the freedom to provide services.

In addition, it should also be considered that the political atmosphere has undoubtedly changed during recent years. Serious action against frauds in insurance adopted by the government together with insurance companies and control authorities as well as the introduction of the 'points system' for driving licenses have reduced the number of accidents and have also limited their costs.

The Italian market is now returning to more acceptable technical results so that even the growth of insurance premiums seems to again be under control and the violation of the duty to insure or the evasion of this duty seem to be less frequent.

§5. THE OBLIGATION TO CALCULATE A CUSTOMIZED ESTIMATE AND PROPOSAL

293. Article 12*bis* of Law No. 990/1969 as amended by Article 22 of Law No. 273/2002 (new rule Title X CAP) establishes that each sales point and Internet site of insurance companies operating in Italy must be able, in all circumstances, to release the following documents and make them available to all users: the pre-contractual information notice; the general and special policy conditions and terms; a free customized estimate drawn up with (a) a specified record number; (b) a validity of not less than sixty days.

The duty to release such a customized estimate is quite large and finds no equals in the economic systems and distribution of financial services: the individual estimate must be made for all types of vehicles and risk over the whole national territory. A regulation to be approved by ISVAP may limit that duty for the future (Article 131 CAP).

§6. THE COVER

294. As seen, motor liability insurance covers the risks of the liability set by Article 2054 CC. In derogation to Article 1917, I comma CC the insured is obliged to pay the victims also in the case of fraud and voluntary act of the driver, absent any chance to act against him/her after the payment.

The insurance is valid also in the case of circulation of the vehicle *prohibente domino* but in this case the coverage is restricted in favour of the victims non-transported or victims transported against their will. In no case is the driver considered a third party able to recover from the insurer.

§7. DIRECT ACTION AGAINST THE INSURANCE COMPANY AND THE LIABLE PARTY

295. Unlike other forms of compulsory insurance, Article 18 L.990/1969 (new rule Article 144 CAP) stipulates the direct action of the victims against the motor liability insurer. More than that, the insurer cannot impose on the victims any exception deriving from the contract.

296. The judicial action of a third party cannot be exercised before sixty days from the formal request to the insurer and with the respect to the procedures provided for the direct indemnification of the victim as provided by Articles 143 et seq. CAP.

In particular it is essential to remember that the *Codice delle Assicurazioni Private* provides a system of *risarcimento diretto* or direct indemnification (Article 149 CAP) thanks to which, if an accident between two or more vehicles occurs, each damaged party can recover the due sum from his/her insurer instead of filing a claim against the insurer of the liable party.

297. This system was previously applied only on a voluntary and conventional basis between the insurance companies which adhered to a special convention (so-called CID or *Convenzione Indennizzo Diretto*). The procedure of *risarcimento diretto*[122] has now become compulsory in all cases where the accident gives place to damages to goods and/or to persons within the limit of biological damage up to 9% of invalidity.

§8. THE RIGHT OF SUBROGATION

298. Article 28 of the Law No. 990/1969 (new rule Article 142 CAP) establishes the right of subrogation of public hospitals and social insurers which have sustained costs from treating the victims of road accidents.

The rule considers the position of public hospitals and other public entities that have anticipated the expenses for the care of the injured (here included are the costs of transport, eventual funeral costs, pharmaceutical costs, etc.). All these entities have the right to be paid directly by the insurer (this is called the principle of direct recovery).

Direct recovery is conditional on the fact that the same costs are not guaranteed by other compulsory insurance and that these entities make their request before the insured has been reimbursed.

299. It should also be remembered that the concrete application of this rule is significantly reduced thanks to the direct reimbursement of the national health care system. The rule is still applicable when the costs have been supported by public entities other than the national health system.

245. The same Article 28 of Law 990/1969 (new rule Article 142) also takes into consideration the position of the social insurers. The subjects to which the rule refers are in particular INAIL (TU No. 1124/1965), and INPS – the national institutes of social insurance. The subrogation applies to the costs sustained by the social insurer and to the indemnity paid to the damaged person.

---

122. A non-exhaustive list of the most important examples of compulsory insurance in Italy would include compulsory insurance for liability for nuclear activities (Law 31 Dec. 1962 No. 1860; compulsory insurance for insurance intermediaries or brokers (Law 1984 No. 792); compulsory insurance for aeronautical products and activities (Law 24 Dec. 1985, No. 808 (Art. 7) D.M. Trasporti 29 Jan. 1999, No. 85; compulsory insurances for gas oil activity and transport (Law 2 Feb. 1973, No. 7 (Arts 5–7)) as well as for hydrocarbons (Law 8 Jul. 1950, No. 640 (Art. 13) – D.P.R. 9 Nov. 1991, No. 404 (Art. 19); compulsory insurance for civil liability of non-profit organizations (Art. 4 Law 11 Aug. 1991 No. 266); compulsory insurance for hunting activities (Law 11 Feb. 1992 No. 57); compulsory insurance for tour operators and agents (Art. 20, Law 17 Mar. 1995 No. 111); compulsory insurance for fiscal auditors and fiscal assistance centres (Law 30 Dec. 1991, No. 413 (Art. 78, c. 6–7); compulsory liability insurance for engineers and building societies in public building contracts (Law 109/1994); compulsory insurance for hospitals (D.P.R. 27 Mar. 1969, No. 130 (Arts 29–30); compulsory insurance for blood transfusions and derivates (D.L. 29 Dec. 1995, No. 553); compulsory insurance for financial societies (Law 2 Jan. 1991, No. 1 (Art. 1 lett. (f))) – Del. CONSOB 2 Jul. 1991, No. 5386 (Art. 16).

We should mention that the activity and functioning of INAIL was established by Law No. 1124 of 30 June 1965. The case in which the two insurances can be involved concerned a case where the negative event was also a work-related accident.

The concept of 'work-related accident' is quite wide, as the case law applies the notion to all accidents if work activity is concerned.

The kind of coverage INAIL is obliged to pay relates to a daily indemnity for inability to work, rent to the beneficiaries, medical costs and prosthesis machines and utilities.

300. Together with INAIL, INPS is the second most important social insurer. Its role is to cover invalidity and pensions. INPS is involved if the car accident gives rise to a right to a disability pension. The right of subrogation consequently arises both from Article 1916 CC and from Article 28 of Law No. 990/1969 (new rule Article 142 CAP).

There are also a number of other minor entities that can benefit from this model of subrogation. Even foreign social insurers benefit from the same right of subrogation under the principle of reciprocity.

With the important decision dated No. 319/1989 the Constitutional Court has declared the rule set by Article 28 of the Law No. 990/1969 (Article 142 CAP) illegitimate in the part that does not establish that the subrogation of the social insurer cannot damage the insured person. Consequently, from that moment on, no pre-deduction from what is due by the liability insurer and in favour of the social insurer can be made to the detriment of the damaged party.

§9. PERSONAL INJURY

301. In general, recovery for personal injury is determined by each court with relevant differences due to the discretionary powers of the judges and the absence of any reference in law.

The legislator consequently intervened in the specific fields of personal injuries deriving from motor accidents with Law No. 75 of 2001. Article 5 of the law disciplines the compensation of personal disabilities by introducing a table of biological indemnity parameters scaled from 1 to 9 (so-called micro-permanent disabilities). The regulations were then completed by the Decree of 3 July 2003 issued by the Ministry of Health and the MAP which issued the table of psycho-physical disabilities.

The Ministry of Productive Business also issued regulations concerning the right of injured persons and the insured to access the settlement documents of motor liability claims after completion of the assessment.

Chapter 3. Other Forms of Liability Insurance

§1. PRODUCT LIABILITY INSURANCE

302. The sources of liability for defective products are found in the D. Lgs. 206/ 2005, *Codice del Consumo* (Code of Consumers) Part. IV, which implemented Directive EC/374/1985 on product liability.

Rules concerning civil liability set by Articles 2043 and 2050 CC as interpreted by the Italian courts still remain applicable, as well as rules deriving from contractual actions set by Article 1491 CC on the contract of sale. The actual situation consequently sees the existence of a concourse of laws even if the discipline set by Code of Consumers is preferred and in most cases is the most favourable to the injured party. An exception is for pharmaceutical products: in fact, as the Code of Consumers contains the so-called risk-development defence, Article 2050 of the Civil Code is preferred as according to this rule

As a consequence of the functioning of this set of rules, strict liability is applied to the producer in case of damage deriving from defective products.

303. Liability insurance for defective products covers the liability set by the law: insurance policies generally make reference to the responsibility of the producer as it is determined according to the law notwithstanding its qualification in terms of contractual liability or liability in tort.

304. Product liability insurance is not compulsory under Italian law. Nonetheless, product liability insurance is very widespread among major Italian producers. The most common policies on the market generally provide for an exclusion of coverage for damage occurring in the USA and Canada, which can be insured with special clauses.

305. Product liability claims have recently increased but their growth is not so dramatic as might be expected. Even the cost of product liability insurance is under control and has not been subject to high increases.

§2. MEDICAL LIABILITY INSURANCE

306. Medical liability is actually oriented towards a very strong protection of the victims of malpractice, both when it derives from a personal liability of the professional and when it depends on a lack in the organization and management of a medical institution.

During recent years medical liability has acquired an autonomous position in the general sector of liability, so that it can be considered a sort of microcosm where some fundamental principles apply with particular reference to Article 32 of the

Italian Constitution, which protects the right of personal safety, and the position of special care towards the persons involved in medical activities.[123]

On the other hand, the complexity of the liability system derives from the fact that professional liability is intersected with the general liability of medical institutions, especially for lack of organization or *intra-moenia* illness.

307. From the juridical point of view, the liability deriving from medical malpractice is actually considered 'trans-typical' in the sense that it shifts from contractual to tort liability and quite often the two are combined.

308. The number of medical malpractice cases has doubled from 1994 to 2002 (from 8000 to 15,000 cases per year). This is mainly due to a change in the community custom, even though we cannot talk about a malpractice crisis comparable to that known some years ago in the USA system. Not only the number but also the cost of accidents has risen. In fact, the average cost of each case has risen 21% in professional liability and 67% in general liability of hospitals and medical institutions. This was mainly due to the rise of the amount of damages awarded to victims, especially for personal damages and pain and suffering.[124]

A number of claims are actually filed against gynaecological activities. In particular we must mention cases of birth following unsuccessful sterilization operations. Here we can identify two different trends of the case law.

309. The first tends to protect in any case the right to a free determination of the woman and of parents. So that even the birth of a perfectly safe child is considered a tort and gives place to the right of economic recovery at least for the necessities of the child. A second judicial trend seems to limit the recovery to cases in which the activity of the doctor has determined the birth of an unsound child. In this case an award is granted to the parents and to the child itself.

310. Premiums of medical liability insurance policies are rising rapidly in proportion to the increasing costs of accidents.

311. An important reform of the medical liability system is actually under discussion in the Italian Parliament. An initial draft was presented by the Parliamentary Commission on Public Heath (Act No. 108 of 21 May 2002). The core of the malpractice reform under discussion is the introduction of a system of strict liability for all public and private institutions performing medical and para-medical activities.

A system of compulsory insurance based on direct action of the victims of medical malpractice towards the medical institutions should complete the introduction of the strict liability rules.

---

123. As can be seen the name has changed from *indennizzo* to *risarcimento*.
124. For a historical outlook see M. Zana, *Responsabilità medica e tutela del paziente* (Giuffé, Milan, 1993).

Chapter 4. Fire Insurance

312. Fire insurance is traditionally offered with a general policy covering all risks relating to property.

Except for public property, fire insurance (for private property) is voluntary. No legal obligation to insure buildings exists or is the responsibility of the owner or the householder unless by a specific agreement in the renting contract.

313. The value of the damage insured by fire insurance coverage is set according to special clauses of the contracts within the limit of the indemnity principle.

Most frequently the parties provide for the clause *valore a nuovo*. In this case the insurer pays the value necessary to acquire or rebuild the property. The clause is considered compatible with the indemnity principle even if the insurer pays a sum which exceeds the value of the property at the time of the accident.

314. The beneficiary of the insured sum is determined and identified in the contract and it may be the owner or even, where a debtor-creditor relation exists, the creditor. In fact, he/she is entitled to a legal privilege on the insured sum if the credit relates to the selling of the property.

It is quite common that he/she is also entitled by a specific agreement to the insured sum.[125]

---

125. See data in *ANIA Annual Report 2004*.

Chapter 5. Credit Insurance, Caution (or Suretyship) Insurance and Consumer Credit Insurance

§1. INTRODUCTION AND SPECIAL PROVISIONS APPLICABLE TO CREDIT RISKS

315. The coverage of credit risk is realized in three main different forms: credit insurance (*assicurazione del credito*); caution (or bond or suretyship) insurance (*assicurazione fideiussoria o cauzionale*); consumer credit insurance (*assicurazione del credito ai consumatori* or *assicurazione prestiti*).

While consumer credit insurance does not correspond to an autonomous branch of activity but merely represents the use of life or personal insurance as a form of indirect guarantee, credit insurance and caution (or bond insurance) are contracts where the coverage directly refers to the credit risk.

The offering of these types of contracts corresponds to the exercise of the activities under branches 14 and 15 of Annex A to the Legislative Decree No. 175/1995 (new rule Article 2 CAP).

In Italy as well as in other European countries the exercise of these branches of activity requires the adoption of particular technical reserves.

316. Special provisions are provided for the exercise of branches 14 and 15 of Annex A to the Legislative Decree 175/1995 (new rule Article 2 CAP) as a consequence of the peculiar character of the credit risk covered by these kinds of policies.

First of all, the exercise of these branches requires the creation of specific technical reserves which have to be monitored by ISVAP. In addition to law requirements derived from the implementation of European directives, ISVAP's Circular Letter No. 162 of 24 October 1991 has imposed on insurance companies respect for a number of other prudential rules which testify once more to the existing link between the discipline of the single contract and the need to see it as a part of a wider and complex activity where risk is treated in a specific way.

317. In particular, the instructions given by ISVAP prohibit the issuing of such coverage on the sole base of fiduciary relations between the insurance company and the debtor, requiring a specific procedure in order to evaluate and price the credit risk.

The control authority's requirements taken together tend to reduce the risk of adverse selection when they require that credit insurance contracts are stipulated for the whole mass of credit positions of the insured (*principio di globalità*) and must establish that a part of the risk remains on the insured (*scoperto obbligatorio*). In order to prevent fraud the control authority also prohibits the commercial credit insurance contract being stipulated by the debtor (even if in the interest of the creditor) so that the sole possible contract scheme sees the creditor as policyholder.[126]

---

126. Candian & Paci (eds), *Manuale di tecnica delle assicurazioni*, ed. D. Cerini & V. Petrone (Milan, 1997), vol. II.

§2. (COMMERCIAL) CREDIT INSURANCE

318. Credit insurance is conventionally divided into two main sectors: the first is internal credit insurance and the second is export credit insurance.

Export credit insurance is exercised with the participation of the SACE insurance company.

Internal credit insurance is mainly offered under the form of commercial credit insurance and it is so-called because the contract relates to commercial activities and the insured risk is that of insolvency of the debtor.

The contract generally contains a special definition of insolvency which is not equal to that provided for public purposes by the Article 5 of the Law on Winding Up (Law No. 267 of 16 March 1942).

319. In fact, commercial credit insurance contracts generally provide that the duty of the insurer to pay arises when the debtor does not pay in due time or when he/she is unable to meet his/her obligation within a fixed period (insolvency in fact).

Despite the fact that the introduction of a conventional definition of insolvency makes the contract resemble a guarantee, it is an insurance contract and it is consequently submitted to the rules set by the Civil Code for insurance contracts (Article 1882 CC) without any derogation.

320. The discipline concerning the declaration of risk set by Articles 1892 and 1893 CC and also the rules referring to aggravation and modification of risk fully apply to credit insurance. Nonetheless, a deeper cooperation between the insurer and the insured is required because it is generally the insurer which makes an exact analysis of the risk and has the professionalism necessary to monitor the debtor's position.

321. Litigation in court for commercial credit insurance is quite low.

§3. CAUTION OR SURETYSHIP INSURANCE CONTRACTS

322. Caution insurance or bonds insurance (the variety of names for guarantees given by insurance companies reflects the wide diversity of contract models offered in the Italian market) can be issued by insurance companies under the authorization for branch No. 15, Annex A to the Legislative Decree No. 175/95 (new rule Article 2 CAP).

Surety bonds and other forms of unnamed guarantees given by insurance companies are not typical contracts.[127]

---

127. See C. Vivante, *Il codice di commercio commentato. Il contratto di assicurazione – di pegno – di deposito nei magazzini generali* (Turin, 1936); U. Navarrini, *Trattato elementare di diritto commerciale*, vol. I, 1932-X, 3rd edn, 344; R. Boccia, 'Evoluzione e trasformazioni dell'assicurazione 'credito'e 'cauzioni'', in *Le assicurazioni del credito e delle cauzioni nel mondo, coll. Quaderno della Rivista Monografica 'Dibattiti rotariani'*, 1974; M. Fragali, *Assicurazione del credito*, in EGI;

Surety bonds and guarantees are submitted to the general contract law contained in Title II of Book IV of the Civil Code and in addition to the existing rules of other legal types of contracts by way of analogy. Obviously, the courts play an important role in the process of normalization and the general tendency of the courts is to apply the rules of the insurance contracts or the rules of the contract of *fideiussione* (*fideiussio*) by way of analogy.[128]

Italian surety bonds generally allow the inclusion of clauses *prima domanda*. This is considered compatible with the requirements set by ISVAP Circular Letter No. 162/1991.

Cautions and bond guarantees offered by insurance companies are very often used in public construction contracts, in particular within the application of the Law No. 109 of 1994 as modified by various subsequent laws (so-called *Legge quadro sui lavori pubblici – Merloni ter* and ff.).

§4. CONSUMER CREDIT INSURANCE

323. Assicurazione del credito ai consumatori or *assicurazione dei prestiti* (consumer credit insurance or loan credit insurance) is the conventional name given to the use of insurance contracts of different branches – in particular life, disability and damage insurance – in order to protect the credit of a third party, which is identified as the specific beneficiary of the insurance contract.

This contractual scheme is mainly promoted by banks and financial institution (society registered under the special register established under Article 107 of Law No. 385/1993 – *Testo Unico Bancario* or TUB) which give credit to their clients and desire to protect that credit with an insurance contract guarantee.

324. From a contractual point of view, the scheme is generally realized thanks to a group or collective insurance stipulated by the creditor (the bank or the financial institution granting the loan) where the debtors are insured and pay the premium. The rent or indemnity sum due by virtue of the insurance contract if the insured event occurs is then attributed to the creditor and only for the part in excess is attributed to the insured itself.

Case law on the matter is quite limited. The lack of controversy does not mean a lack of problems, especially in terms of protection of the insured. In fact the Italian legal system does not have a specific discipline for group insurance and nor are specific provisions set in order to protect the debtor, who is often obliged to stipulate such a contract in favour of the creditor.

G. De Zuliani, *Le assicurazioni del credito e delle cauzioni*, ed. Assicurazioni Generali, 1973; D.Cerini, *Assicurazione e garanzia del credito. Prospettive di comparazione*, Giuffré edn (Milan, 2003).

128. What distinguishes a typical contract from a non-typical contract is the cause of the contract and a complete discipline of the rules governing the contract. Typical contracts are those with a typical *causa*. The Italian legal system permits the conclusion of non-typical contract on the basis of Art. 1322 CC, II paragraph.

325. Consumer credit insurance should not be confused with mortgage insurance which is a financial guarantee that insures lenders against loss if a borrower defaults on a mortgage.

In this case, even though the final beneficiary is always the lender, as in consumer credit insurance policies, the risk covered by the contract is a credit risk and not a risk related to the persons.

Mortgage insurance is not very widespread in Italy and only a few branches of foreign companies offer this contract to banks.

Part IV. Life Insurance and Other Forms of Insurance Related to the Person

Chapter 1. Life Insurance

§1. Types of Life Insurance

326. Life insurance is defined as a contract where the insurer, on payment of a premium, undertakes the duty to pay a capital sum or an annuity upon the happening of an event upon human life (Article 1882 CC).

The rules regulating life insurance are mainly to be found in the Civil Code (Articles 1882–1903, for general rules on insurance, and Articles 1919–1931, especially provided for life insurance contracts). These articles are in fact applicable to insurance schemes that can be qualified as life insurance, while operations other than insurance (i.e., pensions fund related contracts) listed in Article 2 CAP) are excluded.

The traditional notion of the life insurance contract has profoundly changed as a consequence of the spread of non-traditional contracts, on the one hand (especially under the form of financial products with investment risks on the charge of the insured) and also because of the new rules approved as European legislation and in particular the third Life Directive – as implemented by Article 2 CAP).

327. These novelties together have determined (implicit) important exceptions to the local discipline, by providing the right to revoke the proposal and the right of withdrawal after the conclusion of the contract. In addition, the same legislation has obliged insurance companies to give a prior information notice.

There is no doubt that the revised European rules have significantly changed the national approach to life insurance with a sort of re-balancing of the position of the insured *vis-à-vis* the insurance company. This trend has been completed by the detailed provisions approved by ISVAP on life insurance with a series of circular letters concerning information and transparency in the different lines of the life insurance business.

328. For practical reason, the contracts of life insurance are sub-divided into three main forms corresponding to the more widespread actuarial models.[129]

The first is term life insurance (*assicurazioni temporanee caso morte*): here the insured risk is the death of the insured person and the right to payment matures if the death occurs within the period designated in the policy.

The term life insurance may allow the insured to renew the coverage or to convert the coverage into another type of life insurance, such as whole life insurance. In fact, term life insurance is less and less common in Italy, if not in group insurance contracts related to consumer credit.

The second form of insurance is whole life insurance (*assicurazione a vita intera*). In this case the payment matures at the death of the insured whenever that happens. The contract provides the payment of a specified endowment in the form of capital or annuity if the insured survives to a certain date.

The most common form of life insurance is mixed insurance (*assicurazioni miste*). In this form, the policy provides for the payment of a specified amount if the death occurs within a given time; if the insured survives to a specified maturity date, the insured will be paid a specific endowment.[130]

Funds-related insurances fall into this last category. In fact, unit-linked and index-linked policies are more and more widespread in Italy. Because of the presence of the investment risk, insurance companies are required to respect specific duties of information and transparency.

§2. PAYMENT OF PREMIUMS IN LIFE INSURANCE

329. Normally, life insurance is taken for a term of many years. Consequently, it would not be reasonable that the general regulation concerning the failure to pay the premium be applied, since over the years the economic condition of the policy-holder may change. That is why Article 1924 CC provides special rules for the non-payment of premiums in life insurance.

In particular, if the contracting party fails to pay the premium for the first year, the insurer, within six-months from the date of maturity of the premium, can bring an action to obtain performance of the contract. This provision applies even if the payment of the premium is divided into more than one instalment, subject to the provision of the first two paragraphs of Article 1901 CC. In such a case, the six-month period begins to run from the date of maturity of each instalment.

330. On the other hand, if a party fails to pay the subsequent premium within the period of grace provided by the policy or, in the absence of such provision, within twenty days from the date of maturity, the contract dissolves by operation of

---

129. P. Bavaresco, 'Sulla natura giuridica dell'assicurazione fideiussoria: spunti di riflessione dalla dottrina e dalla giurisprudenza', in *DEA*, 1997, 887ff.; C. Botta, 'Le polizze fideiussorie', nella collana *Il diritto privato oggi*, ed. P. Cendon, Milan, 1999.

130. For a comprehensive analysis of life insurance regulation see L. Buttaro, *Assicurazione sulla vita*, *Enciclopedia del diritto*, III, (Milan, 1958); more recently see Polotti I Zumaglia, A. *Assicurazione sulla vita*, *Il diritto delle assicurazioni*, UTET, III, (Turin, 1992). For economic and statistical domestic data see ANIA Annual Report, 2003–2004, in particular 5ff.

law. In this case, the premiums already paid are retained by the insurer unless the conditions exist for the redemption of the insurance or for the reduction of its amount (Article 1924 CC).

§3. REDEMPTION AND REDUCTION OF THE CONTRACT

331. Life insurance contracts allow an accumulation of money that could become useful for the insured before the natural expiry of the contract itself. The insurer cannot give all the money received back nor can he/she allow any restitution, unless the costs of acquisition have been covered and the mathematical reserve has been formed.

For that reason the law, attempting to benefit an insured who becomes unable to continue the payment of the premium or simply decides to interrupt the payment of premiums, permits the reduction (*riduzione*) or redemption (*riscatto*) of the insurance contract under specific conditions.

332. Reduction and redemption of life insurance contracts have very different effects on the contract.

Redemption determines the resolution of the contract and it is on condition that the mathematical reserve has been formed and that the duty of the insurer to pay is not uncertain unless it is due.

The amount of money due in case of redemption is very low compared to the premium paid. In fact, the value in case of redemption is reduced by all costs and expenses for the acquisition of the contract plus a deduction for the mathematical reserve. The redemption ends the insurance contract with the restitution of the value of redemption to the insured.

The effect of the reduction is completely different because in this case the contract remains valid but only for a limited sum. In this case, the contract is modified in order to adjust the debt of the insurer to the premiums paid by the insured.

333. The economic aspects of reduction and redemption of the insurance contract are freely determined by the parties.

Nonetheless, because of the relevant effects of redemption and reduction on the contract, the law requires that the insurance policy clearly regulate the right of redemption and reduction of the amount of the insurance, so that the insured is in a position to know at all times what the redemption or the reduction value of the insurance would be (Article 1925 CC).

334. Redemption is a unilateral declaration which is valid when it arrives with the insurer. It can be in any form, if a special one is not required by the contract.

Because it is considered an act of extraordinary administration, redemption is a personal act of the contracting party and cannot be asked for or exercised by his/her creditors or by the curator.[131]

---

131. In 2003–2004 traditional products saw significant growth after a period of dominance for unit-linked and index-linked policies.

335. It is under discussion whether, in the case of designation of an irrevocable beneficiary, his/her consent is necessary for the valid exercise of the right of redemption.

Some authors consider the consent of the beneficiary as a necessary element. This should be a consequence of the fact that in case of irrevocable designation the beneficiary acquires a direct right against the insurer, so that the latter is obliged to acquire his/her consent to the redemption of the contract.

Others consider that given the personal nature of the right of redemption, the consent of the beneficiary is not necessary, even if the amount paid by the insurer is to be given to the beneficiary.

An intermediate position has finally been proposed. Only if the designation of beneficiary is provided in order to extinguish a debt of a contracting party to the beneficiary is his/her consent necessary.

§4. SPECIFIC DUTIES OF INFORMATION IN LIFE INSURANCE

336. The need for transparency in the wide arena of financial services is increasing in accordance with the disclosure required to financial institutions and with the more careful behaviour of customers in planning their savings. In the light of this new framework, Italian insurers are facing important challenges and innovations introduced by authorities, especially connected with higher disclosure of the underlying risk profile of the assets.

If basic duties of information are provided by the Civil Code with reference to the right of reduction and redemption of the policy (Article 1925 CC mentioned above), Legislative Decree No. 174/1995 enlarged the duty of information and was further implemented by the Code of Private Insurances.

Article 185 of the CAP states that the insurer has a specific pre-contractual duty to inform the insured: the information to be given concerns the insurance company and, in particular, the contract.

Regulation 35/2010 by ISVAP integrate the duty to inform with reference to all life insurance contracts and with specific reference to contracts linked to funds or an index.

§5. CONTRACT ON THE LIFE OF A THIRD PERSON AND CONTRACT FOR THE BENEFIT OF A THIRD PERSON

337. Life insurance can be for one's own life or the life of another person. In this case, in order to avoid the contract becoming an incentive to homicide, the validity of the insurance contract is submitted to the consent of the third party (Article 1919 CC).

338. A different hypothesis is that of a life insurance contract to the benefit of a third party. In this case, the insured sum is devoted to a beneficiary. The designation of the beneficiary can be expressed or generic, for example with reference to the heirs in general, and it can be done at the time of the conclusion of the contract or even later.

339. It should be noted that the designation of the beneficiary is revocable with a declaration of the policyholder. The only case of irrevocable designation is when it is declared non-revocable by the policyholder and the beneficiary has accepted the designation in writing.

In any case, the designation of a beneficiary can be revoked in case of attempts on the life of the insured, in case of ingratitude, or in the case of birth of children. One should also consider that the sum attributed with the insurance contract is not part of the hereditary assets of the policyholder, so that it can be freely assigned.

§6. CHANGES IN THE OCCUPATION OR ACTIVITY OF THE INSURED

340. The rules concerning the aggravation of risk established by Article 1898 CC[132] find a more specific regulation with reference to life insurance.

In particular, Article 1926 CC sets a special rule for the case of change of occupation and activity by the insured. Those changes in the profession or occupation of the insured will not cause the effect of the insurance to cease unless they aggravate the risk to such an extent that, if the new situation had existed at the time the contract was entered into, the insurer would have not agreed to the insurance.

341. When the changes are such that, if the new situation had existed at the time the contract was made, the insurer would have agreed to the insurance for a higher premium, then the payment of the insured sum is reduced in proportion to the lower premium agreed upon, as compared to the premium that would have been required otherwise. If the insured notifies such changes, the insurer in turn should declare within fifteen days whether he/she intends to terminate the contract, reduce the insured amount or increase the premium.

If the insurer states that he/she intends to modify the contract in one of the ways mentioned above, the insured should declare within fifteen days whether he/she intends to accept the offer or not. If the insured does not accept, the contract is terminated without prejudging the insurer's right to the premium for the current period of insurance and the right of the insured to the redemption of the contract. The silence of the insured would be construed as acceptance. The notification and declaration can be made by registered mail.

342. This rule has to be interpreted in the reasonable sense that the insured is not obliged to maintain his/her habits or profession unaltered and it only regulates changes. Besides, most authors consider only the professional occupation as relevant for Article 1926 CC.[133] Other authors, on the other hand, tend to consider

132. Cass. 28 Jul. 1965 No. 1811.
133. See above, Part II.

relevant also non-occasional changes of the activity of the insured, both professional and relative to sports, etc.[134]

The case law employs the rule set for the interpretation of Article 1898 CC, concluding that only non-transitory and occasional changes are relevant.[135]

One should remember that, according to Article 1932 CC, Article 1926 CC can be derogated only in favour of the insured and most policies state the irrelevance of the change of profession of the insured, if not for some specific situations (i.e., military activity in war time).

§7. THE SUICIDE OF THE INSURED

343. Article 1927 CC provides that if the insured commits suicide within two years from the making of the contract, the insurer is not bound to pay the insured sum, unless otherwise agreed. In addition, the insurer is likewise not bound to pay it, in the event of the contract being suspended for non-payment of premiums, two years have not elapsed from the day on which the suspension ceased (so-called *periodo di carenza*).

The rule, according to the will of the parties, can be modified in such a way as to enable the immediate coverage of the suicide or to exclude coverage even after the two-year period.

344. Article 450 in the abrogated Commercial Code 1882 established an equivalence between suicide and death for gross negligence of the insured as a rule for the exclusion of the coverage.

The actual formulation of Article 1927 CC does not contain a similar equivalence. Some authors have instead proposed the application of the general rule set by Article 1900 CC, which excludes coverage for fraud or gross negligence. According to other authors, the special character of Article 1927 CC makes it predominant over the general rule of Article 1900, even in light of the consideration that suicide represents a voluntary act, so that gross negligence is consequently included in the derogation. The case law fully adheres to this more favourable interpretation.

345. Obviously, the case disciplined by Article 1927 CC provides for a special case of *dolus* of the insured that commits suicide, but in any case it does not deal with the *dolus* of the beneficiary implicated in the homicide and therefore it is not covered by the contract under any conditions (also in application of Article 1900 CC).

This rule is also stressed by Article 1922, according to which the designation of the beneficiary, even if irrevocable, is not effective if the beneficiary makes an attempt on the life of the insured. If the designation is irrevocable and it is made as an act of liberality or gift, it can be revoked in the cases set out in Article 801 CC.

---

134. Candian & Polotti Di Zumaglia-Gasparoni, *Contratti di assicurazione vita. Infortuni, Contratti para-assicurativi* (Milan, 1993), 54.
135. Donati & Volpe Putzolu, *Manuale di diritto delle assicurazioni private* (Milan, 2003), 192.

346. Suicide is seen as an exclusion of coverage. Therefore, the burden of proving that the insured died of suicide lies on the insurer, according to the general principle of Article 2697 CC.

§8. THE PROTECTION OF THE INSURED SUMS FROM EXECUTION

347. A fundamental rule in life insurance is that of Article 1923 CC, according to which no execution can be levied on sums due by the insurer to the contracting party or to the beneficiary, and nor can these sums be subjected to provisional remedies.

The policy of this rule – which is not applicable to non-life insurance – is to be found in the intention to favour the accumulation of money for the welfare, thanks to the use of life insurance. In fact, the rule was already set by Article 453 of the Commercial Code of 1882. It provided, in case of conflict between the beneficiary of a life insurance contract and the creditors of the insured, preference for the beneficiary.

348. Nevertheless, two important principles limit the practical application of the 'protection rule'. The first regards the fact that the provisions concerning collation, imputation or reduction of gifts remain applicable with respect to the premiums already paid. In other words, creditors and heirs can act for the restitution of the sums that have been paid as premiums. When the action is made by the creditors, they are allowed to obtain revocation as provided by Article 2901 CC. This rule provides in fact for a action to prevent the diminution of the debtor's estate by his/her fraud.

349. According to Article 2901 CC this action can be exercised if some conditions are present.

First, the debtor must have been aware of the prejudice which the act would cause to the rights of creditors or, if the act was prior to the existence of the claims, that the act was fraudulently designed for the purpose of damage the satisfaction of the claim. Second, in case of a non-gratuitous act, the third person involved must have been aware of the said prejudice or of the fraudulent design. In the presence of the said elements, the creditor, after having secured a declaration of ineffectiveness of the act, can institute against third person transferees enforcement proceedings or proceedings to secure precautionary measures on the property that was the object of the act in question.

350. The second limitation concerns the time of the execution. In fact, the protection of the sums operates only until they are kept by the insurer (the rule literally refers to the *somme dovute* – due sums). After the payment, the sums from the insurance contract are confused with the assets of the receiver, so that Article 1923 CC becomes ineffective.[136]

---

136. Cass. 10 Apr. 1987 No. 3563 in *Assicurazioni*, 1988, II, 23.

A recent case held by the Supreme Court[137] has provided a partially different interpretation of the rule. In particular the Supreme Court stated that the protection of the sums due to the beneficiary was applicable only if the insurance contract had reached its natural expiry. In particular the Supreme Court reasoned its decision starting from the assumption that the legal *ratio* of Article 1923 is to protect and guarantee the social security function of life insurance contract, and that this scope will only be considered reached when the contract comes to its natural expiration date.[138]

---

137. Cass. 3 Dec. 1988, No. 6548.
138. Cass. 26 Jun. 2000, No. 8676.

Chapter 2. The Contract of Capitalization (or Capital Redemption)

351. The contract of capitalization is an economic operation through which the interest matured in a capital sum adds to and becomes capital itself.

352. The contract of capitalization is considered as a branch of the insurance activity within the sector of life insurance (see Article 2 CAP). Nonetheless, from a contractual point of view, the capitalization is a non-nominated contract and it does not belong to the contract of insurance because of the lack of demographic risk. In fact, the capitalization contract is a financial operation where the duty of the insurer is not linked to facts related to human life.

That means that the operation, even if permissible for insurance companies, is not submitted to the rules of Article 1882 CC ff.

353. In the lack of a detailed regulation of the contract of capitalization, the legal doctrine has suggested the application (by use of the analogical process) of the rules set by Articles 1882 et seq., with the sole exception of those concerning the demographic risk.[139] According to other authors, the rules relating to insurance contracts and compatible with the capitalization contract are, on the contrary, to be determined case by case.[140]

---

139. For further details see S. Nitti, *Polizze vita: declino dell'impignorabilità?* in DEA, 2001, 193.
140. Donati & Volpe Putzolu, *Manuale delle assicurazioni private*, 2003, Ch. XIX.

Chapter 3. Pension Funds and the Pension System

354. Italy is no exception to the crisis of the public pension system, as a consequence of the increased life expectancy of the population and the insufficiency of the individual and collective schemes with reference to the increasing age of the population. For this reason many reforms have been recently adopted both in the public system of the pension funds and in private collateral schemes. In addition, the need to comply with the economic Maastricht requirements related to GDP has strengthened the need for a structural reform.[141]

§1. THE FIRST PILLAR: PUBLIC PENSION SCHEMES

355. The Italian pension system is almost entirely composed of a compulsory public system that is financed through a cumulative contribution system. The public system is nonetheless fragmented because of the coexistence of over fifty different schemes. The five largest schemes cover about four-fifths of total pension expenditure. Most of the other schemes involve very few workers or pensioners.

More than two-thirds of the public pension system is administered by INPS (Social Security Institute for the private-sector). It insures the largest part of private-sector employees and the self-employed (artisans, farmers and shopkeepers). About quarter of the public pension system is administered by INPDAP (Social Security Institute for the public sector), and the remaining part is administered by a number of small institutions.[142]

356. The legal–institutional framework of the Italian public pension system has been heavily reformed over the last decade. In particular, three main reforms have been adopted, respectively in 1992 (Legislative Decree No. 503/92 – Amato reform), 1995 (Law No. 335/95 – Dini reform) and 1997 (Law No. 449/97 – Prodi reform), which provide a process moving towards a new regime – the 'contribution-based regime'. In addition to these, we should mention the disability pension reform approved in 1984 (Law No. 222/84), which significantly reduced the number of newly awarded pensions, and which is still producing effects in terms of a reduction of the outstanding stock of pensions.[143]

In particular, following the 1995 reform (Law No. 335/95), the Italian pension system is moving gradually to a new regime applied to all labour-market entrants

---

141. A.D. Candian, *I contratti para-assicurativi,* in AA.VV., *Contratti di assicurazione vita. Infortuni, Contratti para-assicurativi,* Milan, 1993.
142. For any further details see F. Vallacqua & L. Gabrielli, *The Italian pension system, present structure and prospects, Work in progress,* No. 4, 2003.
143. The relevant ones are: the Journalists Pension Institute (INPGI), the Entertainment Industry Employees Pension Organization (ENPALS), the Industry Managers Pension Institute (INPDAI), the state railway's funds, the postal and telecommunications services. In addition, there is a long list of bodies that manage the funds of freelance categories. For more details, see the full report by Ministero del Wealfare (2002), *Gli andamenti finanziari del sistema pensionistico obbligatorio,* Rome.

after 31 December 1995. The main feature of this regime concerns the method of calculation.

357. In very brief terms, the new system takes into account both the amount of contribution paid throughout the whole working life (capitalized at the rate of nominal GDP) and the life expectancy of the pensioner at retirement age (and the number of years during which any widow or widower will be able to collect survivor's benefits) according to actuarial equivalences.

Thus, benefits strongly relate to retirement age – the lower the age, the lower the pension and vice versa. Retirement age was temporally ranged from 57 to 65, but workers may not retire earlier than 65 unless they have reached a pension level of at least 1.2 times the old age allowance. In all cases, at 65 people will be at least entitled to such benefit, if they are not able to earn any other income (pensions included).

A further reform (Law No. 243/2004) has finally eliminated age flexibility by reintroducing a fixed system of age requirement of 60 years and 65 years respectively for women and men.

358. The new regime will be fully phased in after 2030–2035. Meanwhile, there will be a transition period that only affects workers already employed at the end of 1995.

According to the current legal framework, the possibility for a pensioner to add the amount of his/her pension to other income is limited in some cases and forbidden in others. It mainly depends on the category of pension (disability, seniority or old age), the kind of income (employed or self-employed activity), the years of contribution matured (less or more than 40) and the regime (earning-related, mixed or contribution based).

It is worth noting that, during recent years, the legislation has been constantly improved in order to reduce barriers to the extension of work as pensioner.

359. Eligibility requirements are gradually increasing for workers involved in the transition period. As far as the old age pension is concerned, a minimum age of 65 for men and 60 for women is required and a joint minimum contribution period of 20 years starting from 2001. At the same time, eligibility requirements for a seniority pension will be increased significantly. To qualify, different requirements of age are determined with reference to sex (male or female) and to public or private nature of the employer.

§2. THE SECOND PILLAR: COLLECTIVE PRIVATE FUNDED PENSION SCHEMES

360. The 1990s have seen the reform and consequently the development of a complementary system, necessary to compensate the effective long-term for trend to reduce public pensions.

361. Stressing the role of the complementary system, the primary need to define a specific and organic regulatory design emerged. Indeed, before Law No. 421/

1992, the forms of the collective integrative pension system were limited to specific slices of the labour-market. They were characterized by higher-than-average contributions (banks, insurance companies, managers) and they operated according to common law regulations (not always consistent with the peculiar configuration of pension funds – and some general rules specifically aimed at this sector (Articles 2117 and 2123 CC) – although concerning limited aspects) and some dispositions relative to specific types of pension fund.

The structural aspects – such as the juridical form of pension funds, management models, performance models and the relationship with the compulsory system and so on – were assigned exclusively to the self-legislation of the supporters of forms of private pensions.

362. Legislative Decree No. 124/1993 and its following modifications and integrations, among which those introduced by Law No. 335/1995 are very important, have introduced a structured discipline of pension forms complementary to the compulsory public system, aiming at ensuring higher levels of pension coverage (*al fine di assicurare più elevati livelli di copertura previdenziale*, Article 1, Legislative Decree 124/93).

363. The discipline approved in 1993 and lately in 2004 was thus aimed at favouring the voluntary constitution of complementary pension systems, both collective and individual, in all production sectors and for all working categories, private and public, employed or self-employed.

In particular, in order to increase the adoption of complementary pension schemes, Law No. 243/2004 has introduced the method of the so-called silence agreement thanks to which the TFR (severance indemnity) is automatically invested in complementary systems.

§3. THE THIRD PILLAR: INDIVIDUAL PLANS

364. It is commonly considered that the third pillar of pension schemes is represented by individual life insurance contracts. Actually they are stipulated under the specific regulation of Articles 9*bis* and 9*ter* of Legislative Decree No. 124/1993 as amended by Legislative Decree No. 47/2000.

Chapter 4. Insurance for Damage to Persons

§1. INTRODUCTION

365. Insurance for damage to persons – in the form of accident insurance and health insurance – does not receive any specific attention by the legislator unless it is given by a public institution (such as INAIL).

Insurances for damage to persons are part of insurance against damage. Nonetheless, legal doctrine tends to identify insurance for damage to persons as a sort of *tertium genus* between life insurance, on the one hand, and non-life insurance, on the other hand. This perspective finds its explanation mainly with reference to the impossibility of applying a number of rules and provisions concerning non-life insurance contracts to cases where the person is involved. Case law adheres to this interpretation by applying by way of analogy rules pertaining to life insurance and damages insurance combined together.

§2. NON-'TRADITIONAL' FORMS OF INSURANCE FOR DAMAGE TO PERSONS: LONG-TERM CARE, FATAL ILLNESS AND INCOME PROTECTION INSURANCE

366. Long-term care refers to a broad range of supportive medical, personal and social services needed by people who are unable to meet their basic living needs for an extended period of time, such as inability to move, dress, bathe, eat, use a toilet, medicate and avoid incontinence. This may be caused by accident, illness or old age.[144]

367. Insurance policies provide a range of benefits or services to cover this disability. This cover is relatively new to the Italian market. If the Civil Code does not provide any rules with reference to the long-term insurance, Decree No. 47/2000 has established a range of requirements and conditions of the contract, for fiscal purposes.

Long-term insurance can be packaged as a stand-alone, that is to say as a comprehensive coverage policy as well as a rider to life insurance policy or to a health insurance policy (*assicurazioni infortuni e malattia*). In the first case these plans

---

144. This law concerned disability pensions related to contributions and, therefore, included in the public pension system. The aim of the reform was to tighten the requirements for being entitled to the benefit, making its granting subject exclusively to the physical and psychological conditions of applicants. Previously, in fact, the requirements for claiming disability pensions could also be assessed taking into account the economic environment. Because of this, disability pensions had frequently been used as a means of obtaining access to a pension with less strict eligibility requirements than for seniority and old age pensions. Consequently, the scope for retiring early in this way has been considerably reduced, as can be seen from the sharp reduction in the number of disability pensions awarded over time. Besides, according to the new legislation, two kinds of disability pensions were introduced depending on whether the reduction of ability to work was up to 60% (*assegno di imobilità*) or 100% (*pensione di invalidità*). The former is subject to a three-year check and allows the pensioner to go on working. The latter is incompatible with labour income while the calculation rules are more generous and provide extra contributions (generally up to the maximum that the pensioner would have been able to reach).

cover all long-term care service and are usually purchased with premiums which are paid for the life of the insured. In the second case the policy represents two separate coverages and the premium is split up to pay for both.

368. Fatal illness and income protection insurance contracts are not regulated by the Civil Code. Fatal illness insurance provides a capital benefit if the policy-holder is diagnosed to have suffered from a number of predefined illnesses or medical conditions and then survives until the end of a short waiting period.

The cover is mainly sold in the market as a rider to a whole life insurance.

Income protection insurance, which covers the risk of illness of the policyholder, is not widespread in the market.[145]

---

145. For further details see V. Petrone, 'Il rischio di non autosufficienza delle persone e le assicurazioni long-term care', in *Il rischio di non autosufficienza e l'offerta assicurativa in Italia*, 2003; E. Pitacco, 'Le copertura assicurative', in DEA, 1992, 345; ISVAP, *Long-Term Care. Le prospettive per il mercato italiano. Due modelli a confronto: Germania e Stati Uniti*, 1998.

Part V. Reinsurance and Co-insurance

Chapter 1. Co-insurance

369. Co-insurance is a widely used technique to spread big risks. A unique rule is provided by the Italian law for co-insurance, in the sense that when the same insurance or the insurance against risks relating to the same property is divided among more than one insurer in a specific share, each insurer is liable for the payment of the indemnity only in proportion to his/her respective share, even if there is only one contract signed by all insurers (Article 1911 CC).

This is in fact the legal assumption of the rule of divisible obligations (*obbligazioni parziarie* – Article 1295 CC). As a consequence, Article 1911 CC implies a unitary objective structure for the insurance, in relation to the same risk and the same insurance conditions; from a subjective point of view, the operation is compound, since each insurer responds according to its own share. Among insurers, therefore, there is no joint liability.[146]

370. Quite often the co-insurance contract provides for an agency power conferred on one of the co-insurers (*clausola di delega*). The clause as agreed between the parties will determine the extension of the agency power conferred on the representative company (*delegataria*) with all the relevant consequences under law, i.e., if the clause involves the power of receiving all contract notifications by the insured, without any limits, sending the register letter to the *delegataria* will interrupt the prescription towards all co-insurers.[147]

---

146. For further details see Pitacco, *supra*, 345ff.
147. Cass. 22 May 1963 No. 1321; Cass. 14 Mar. 1999, No. 1830.

Chapter 2. Reinsurance

371. Reinsurance,[148] as well as co-insurance, is one way in which a risk can be divided between insurers. Thus, the techniques applied in order to reach this goal are very different in the two models.

The main difference is that in co-insurance the risk is taken *pro quota* by different insurers, while in reinsurance the risk is directly taken by only one insurer who, subsequently transfers and distributes the risk or part of it to another insurer. As a consequence, the insured remains outside the contract and the reinsurance contract does not create any relation between the insured and the re-insurer.

372. First of all, it must be clarified that reinsurance is not a special class of business to which a specific authorization corresponds, but it is a special kind of insurance transaction.

Not surprisingly, only a few rules are dedicated to the reinsurance contract in the Civil Code (Articles 1928, 1929, 2952 comma II). The same attitude towards reinsurance was adopted by the superseded Commercial Code of 1882.

Consequent on this lack of regulation for the reinsurance contract, there are different opinions as to the nature of the contract. In particular, some authors consider it as an insurance of the insurer: from this perspective the discipline of the insurance contract is fully applicable. Some other authors conclude that the absence of a specific reference to the discipline of the insurance contract demonstrates that we are not dealing with an insurance contract and consequently exclude the application of this discipline.

373. In any case, these doubts are mainly theoretical rather than practical because there is a general consent by insurers and a case law trend towards the application of most of the rules concerning the insurance contract.[149] In fact the number of reported cases concerning reinsurance issues is relatively small. Briefly, the case law applies to reinsurance contracts the general rules concerning contracts (Articles 1321 et seq. CC), plus the contract clauses and the uses. A few rules concerning insurance are considered applicable to reinsurance thanks to the analogical process. Only a few articles are specifically dedicated to reinsurance.

374. Among the few rules provided for reinsurance is Article 1928 CC: it provides the rule according to which the contract of reinsurance has to be proved in writing. The usual name of this text is 'treaty of reinsurance'. The treaty involves a commitment of a re-insurer to assume part of the risk of the ceding insurer, either on a *pro-rata* basis or an excess basis.

375. Article 1929 CC prevents a reinsurance contract giving way to a direct connection between the re-insurer and the insured. This rule represents an application of the more general principle that the contract does not create any effects over third

---

148. See Cass. 13 Feb. 1980 No. 1038 in FI, 1981, I, 226.
149. R. Capotosti, *La riassicurazione. Il diritto delle assicurazioni*, 2 (Turin, 1991); M. Prosperetti & E.A. Apicella, *La riassicurazione* (Milan, 1994).

parties as set by Article 1372 CC: therefore the reproduction of this principle, while talking about reinsurance, has the special aim of avoiding the connection between the contracts and refusing the thesis of the complex contract which was once proposed in order to create legal duties of the re-insurer towards the insured. In other words, the principle set by Article 1929 CC is intended to maintain complete independence between the insurance and the reinsurance contract.

376. The importance of this independence is confirmed by the fact that Article 1929 CC is mandatory. For all other aspects, the legislator prefers to leave the concrete discipline to the freedom of contract of the parties. In fact the contract of reinsurance does not create any relationships between the insured and the re-insurer, except for the provisions of special laws concerning privileges in favour of a policyholders group.

377. The limitation period in reinsurance is two years (Article 2952 CC comma 2) instead of one year as provided in other insurance contracts.

Chapter 3. Insurance Pools for Specific Risks such as Environmental Risks

378. The insurance pool is a group of insurers that agree to jointly underwrite a series of risks in a particular class of insurances. In Italy, a pool for catastrophic risks and environmental risks has been created. The Pool is coordinated by ANIA (National Association of Insurers).

The creation of a private pool for terrorist risk is currently under discussion. The creation of the pool is related to the eventual coverage by the state of the losses exceeding a certain amount.

Part VI. Insurance Intermediaries

Chapter 1. The Insurance Intermediation System: A Short Historical Outlook

379. Insurance intermediaries are a vital link in the process of selling insurance products and when offering connected services.

They also play an important role in protecting the interests of insurance customers, primarily by offering them advice and assistance and by analysing their specific needs. In simple words, they are a major element in the functioning of the single European market for insurance. This is confirmed by the fact that in Italy, as well as in other markets, distribution and selling of insurance products through intermediaries has always prevailed over direct sale by the insurance companies.[150]

This general trend is expected to change because of a more mature approach to the market by the insurance companies more consistent with consumer protection policies. On the one hand insurers aim to improve their image and to enhance consumers' confidence in financial services; in addition the evolution of distance selling techniques seems to allow insurance companies to acquire more visible areas in the distribution chain without the necessity to open market points on the territory.[151]

This does not mean that insurance intermediaries will disappear, especially in the light of a more complex market, because of the coexistence of diversified products and of local and foreign companies operating under the freedom of services and of establishment. The role of insurance intermediaries will nonetheless have to change into a more sophisticated and attentive activity of assistance to the client, in order for the insurance to be a 'service' and not merely a 'product' to be sold.

380. Despite the importance of the role of insurance intermediaries as the essential link between insurance companies and their clients, the Italian situation has been marked by a long period of substantial absence of regulation of their activity.

This period of substantial lack of regulation stretched from medieval times, when a prototype of the 'intermediary man' made its appearance on the scene (and was

---

150. Donati & Volpe Putzolu, *Manuale delle assicurazioni private*, 249.

151. It should be pointed out that the model of 'intermediate selling' determined through the years involved a neat separation and lack of communication between the insurance companies, from the one side, and their clients, from the other; the possibility for insurance companies to acquire a true perspective of the need of the clients was consequently inevitably restricted so that the confidence of consumers fell.

then called *sensale*), up to the last decades of the twentieth century,[152] when finally Law No. 49/1979 on insurance agents and, some years later, Law No. 792/1984 on insurance brokers were approved in order to give implementation to the first Directive on insurance intermediaries (Directive EC/77/92 of 13 December 1976). In particular the laws led to the creation of the *albi* (registers) for agents and brokers.

§1.   THE IMPLEMENTATION OF DIRECTIVE 2002/92/EC ON INSURANCE
      MEDIATION IN THE CODICE DELLE ASSICURAZIONI PRIVATE

381.   More recently, the legal framework for insurance intermediaries has been completely re-visited thanks to the implementation of the second Directive on insurance intermediaries (Directive EC/2002/92) with the approval of the *Codice delle Assicurazioni Private*, Title IX, from Articles 106–121.
The pillars of the reform can be summarized as follows:

(1) the adoption of a broad definition of insurance intermediaries in line with Article 2 of the second Directive. In fact Article 106 CAP provides that the activity of being an insurance intermediary consists of presenting and proposing insurance and reinsurance products, as well as of giving assistance and consultancy in preparation of such contracts or of assisting in the administration and performance of such contracts;
(2) the creation of a single register for all intermediaries (Article 109 CAP). In particular Article 109 CAP provides that the register is divided into five sections, specifically dedicated to each single category of intermediary and organized as follows:

    – section (a) insurance agents;
    – section (b) insurance and reinsurance brokers; – section (c) free producers;
    – section (d) banks, investment companies and *Poste Italiane–divisione bancoposta* (bank departments of post offices);
    – section (e) any other subject who cooperates with the above-mentioned intermediaries; (quite unexpectedly, the final text of Article 109, last comma CAP prohibits registration under different sections of the register);
    – the acceptance of the principle of the single European passport for all insurance intermediaries (Article 116 CAP);
    – the requirements of professional skills and good repute for all insurance intermediaries (Articles from 110 to 112 CAP); the specific standard of professional skills will have to be determined by ISVAP with further regulations;
    – the fixation of duties and responsibilities of insurance companies and intermediaries for the damages deriving from the activity of the intermediaries (Article 119) as well as of information requirements (Article 120);

---

152. The 're-acquisition' of the client portfolio has been confirmed by recent data, especially with reference to new insurance companies operating in the distance selling market.

- In particular, Article 120, first comma CAP introduces the notion of 'disclosure of independence' according to which the intermediary has to declare his/her position towards the insurance company with reference to the existence of a duty to sell or the existence of any other contractual obligation or relation. This duty applies to all intermediaries. If the insurance intermediary declares itself independent, it has to give a consultancy based on the analysis of a certain number of insurance contracts in the market. In addition, all intermediaries are required to specify and suggest to the client a product that is 'adequate' (*adeguato*) to his/her needs, according to what the client has declared (so-called *dovere di adeguatezza* – Article 120, comma 3 CAP).
- ISVAP is nevertheless required to establish the rules of presentation and information, according to the different needs of protection for consumers, to the specific professional skill of the intermediary and the type of insured risk (Article 120, comma 4 CAP);
- the duty to establish a separate and segregated account for premiums paid to the intermediary by the insured and for all sums collected by the insurance intermediary to be paid to the insured or beneficiary third parties (Article 117). In particular the law established that the fund is not subject to executive action, by subjects other than insured and beneficiaries of insurance undertakings in the limit of the sums due to those persons; in addition, neither legal nor judiciary compensation can operate on the fund; equally, voluntary compensation cannot be agreed between the intermediary and the one who deposits a sum into the fund (Article 117, comma 3 CAP);
- special rules for the effectiveness of payments to the intermediary: in particular
- Article 118, first comma CAP provides that the payment of a premium made in good faith by the insured to the intermediary or to his/her auxiliaries is considered made to the insurance company. Unless the contrary is proved by the insurance company or the intermediary, the sums due to the insured or beneficiary parties is not considered paid if not under subscription of a written receipt by the entitled persons. A partially different regime operates for the broker: in fact the rule provided by Article 118, first comma CAP is applicable to insurance brokers only if provided in a special agreement between the insurance company and the broker; besides the insurance broker is obliged to inform the client about the existence of such an agreement (Article 118, second comma CAP).

382. According to Article 355 CAP, ISVAP will approve regulations to integrate the legislative rules within twenty-four months after the entry into force of the Code (not later than 31 December 2007). Until the adoption of these rules, the old ones will remain into force if not incompatible with the new ones.

After clarifying these preliminary aspects on the implementation of the second Directive, it is necessarily to deal briefly with certain aspects of the evolution of the intermediary activity and legal framework, in order to understand the problems of coordination between the new and the old legal systems.

383. The starting point dates back to the activity of the so-called *sensali*, that is to say those subjects who sold the risk between the potential underwriters.

Over the years the indistinct activity of the *sensale* led to a division between those intermediaries tied with insurers, then called agents, and those who were agents of more than one insurer and, thanks to this wider independence and autonomy from a single principal, could be closer to the clients' needs and were later on called brokers.

At that time a number of collateral figures were present on the intermediary scene, in particular free producers. None of these figures received any specific regulation or restriction by law, in line with the principle of the free market.

This substantial lack of regulation of the intermediary activity continued until the twentieth century.

384. A very few rules were approved at the beginning of 1900: their aim was mainly to regulate the agent–company relation in order to protect economic rights of the agents (and eventually sub-agents) without paying any attention to the idea of protecting the clients' position.

385. When Italy faced the problem of implementing European legislation on insurance intermediaries, in particular Directive EC/77/92 of 13 December 1976, two public registers (*albi*) of intermediaries were created and submitted to the control of the Minister of Industry and Commerce, at first, and ISVAP, a few years later. The first one is the register of insurance agents (established by the Law No. 48/1979) and the second one is the register of insurance brokers (Law No. 792/1984).

From that time, the exercise of the agent or broker activities by those not-registered became a criminal offence under Article 348 of the Criminal Code.

386. Another consequence of the creations of public registers was that from that time on, the perspective and priorities of the approach to insurance mediation dramatically changed.

In the panorama of insurance intermediaries – where agents and brokers seemed to be the only figures able to do intermediary activities and allowed to deal with the clients in the process of the distribution chain – the courts were called on to distinguish quite clearly the position and role of agents and brokers from that of any other not-registered subjects by limiting the role of the latter in the insurance distribution process to very restricted and material activities. In other words, the consequence of the register system deriving from the Law No. 48/1979 and Law No. 792/1984 was the perception of a sort of close market of intermediary activities.

387. Since then, much water has passed under the bridge. It took some years to admit the legitimate role of not-registered intermediaries, assuming that their activity should remain confined to specific activities (in general material activities) with no possibility for them to give consultancy to clients or to have any power of representing the companies.

388. It was then that the control authorities – with ad hoc statements and letters – clarified in particular the legitimate presence in the insurance selling process of banks and investment companies, given that their activity should not correspond to that of agents and brokers. Consequently, the Ministry of Industry and Commerce (Circular Letter No. 502 of 3 February 1986), ISVAP and Bank of Italy (Note of 12 June 1988) expressly clarified their position saying that the sale of insurance products by banks and investment companies was to be considered legitimate if their activity was limited to the offering of standardized products, without any power to represent the insurance companies.

389. Step by step, the attention of the supervisory authorities and of the legislator itself seems to have shifted from the problem of limiting the access to the intermediary market to the need of the insurance distribution process to be marked by a fair and transparent approach, notwithstanding the status and name of the subject doing the activity. This approach seems to be more coherent with the new model coming from the adoption of the second Directive on Insurance intermediaries (Directive EC/2002/92).

390. Actually, there are three major figures of insurance intermediaries in Italy: insurance agents, insurance brokers and banks, immediately followed by the growing presence of investment companies. While agents and brokers are still considered and named 'institutional intermediaries' because of their registration in public lists, banks and investment societies are generally referred to as 'alternative distribution channels'.

Chapter 2. The Insurance Agent

§1. SOURCES OF LAW

391. The agent is historically the insurance intermediary who acts in favour of the insurance company by excellence.

The rules governing the insurance agency scheme and the relation between the agent and the insurance company, on the one hand, and the clients, on the other hand, are to be found in the general laws concerning the contract of agency set by Articles 1751 et seq. of the Civil Code, in Law 1979 No. 48 (new rule Articles 107 et seq. CAP) and in national collective agreements stipulated between ANIA (the Association of Insurance Companies) and the most representative agents' associations, such as in particular the so-called ANA (which stands for Accordo Nazionale Agenti) 2003. In addition, the individual contract stipulated between the single agent and the insurance company completes the set of specific terms of the agent--company relation.

392. It is not always clear how the enumerated sources of law combine. The general rule is in fact that the Civil Code regulation applies if not derogated by collective agreements, on the one hand, and by most favourable individual clauses, on the other hand (Article 1753 CC).

In practical terms, the application of this rule is more complicated. With the exception of specific fields of conflicts of regulations, the collective agreements mainly consider the economic relation between the parties and the causes of resolution of the agreement, while the main rules concerning the position and responsibility of the agent towards the clients and the insurance company are to be found in the Civil Code dispositions. So that at this level the solution is quite simple. Besides, courts are often called to decide whether individual contracts derogating to rules coming from the Civil Code or the collective agreements have the effect of introducing either a more favourable or a detrimental solution for the agent. The case must be decided according to the general principle adopted in labour law cases which states that the evaluation must be made in specific terms and not merely according to the formal application of the rules in question.

§2. DEFINITION OF INSURANCE AGENT ACTIVITY

393. The general definition of the *contratto di agenzia* (contract of agency) is to be found in Article 1742 CC:

> by the contract of agency one party permanently undertakes for a remuneration, to promote the making of contracts for the account of another person within a specified territory.

394. This rule enumerates the essential elements of the agency contract: the stability of the relation between the principal and the agent, on the one hand, and the fiduciary character of their relation, on the other.

The principles obviously apply to all contracts of agency including those between insurance companies and their agents. In the fiduciary character of the relation between the insurance company and the agent lies the major difference from the role of the broker who is an independent intermediary.

§3. THE RELATION BETWEEN THE PRINCIPAL AND THE AGENT

395. According to Article 1743 CC the principal cannot employ more than one agent at the same time in the same area and in the same line of business, nor can the agent undertake business transactions in the same area and in the same line for the account of more than one of the enterprises in competition with each other. This is called the *diritto di esclusiva* (the different regimes of exclusiveness are better specified in collective agreements).

396. Another important rule applying to the insurance agency contract is that the agent, unless a different agreement exists, does not have the power to represent the insurance company.

A partial derogation to this rule is set by the law itself. In fact, according to Article 1745 CC, all declarations concerning performance of the contract entered into through the agent and all complaints relating to non-performance of the contract can validly be made to the agent.

397. The rule is completed by the special provision concerning the insurance contract execution set by Article 1903 CC dealing with the modification or dissolution of the insurance contracts. Agents who are authorized to make such contracts can perform all acts that are within the scope of the authority contained in the power of attorney published with the formalities required by law.

Such agents can also institute actions and be made defendants in the name of the insurer, in proceedings connected with obligations arising from the acts done in the performance of their agency before the courts of the place in which the office of the contracting agency is located.

398. According to Article 1748 CC, the agent is entitled to receive commission for all transactions that have been regularly completed when the transaction is entered into as a consequence of his/her intervention. Commission is due also for transactions entered into by the principal with third parties that the agent had previously acquired as clients for transactions of the same kind or pertaining to the area or category or group of clients reserved to the agent, unless otherwise agreed.

399. The discipline is then to be completed by the specific rules coming from the special legislation for insurance, i.e., Law No. 48/1979 (new rule Title IX of the CAP and further laws to be approved under Article 355 CAP), and the collective agreements. Three major collective agreements were approved: the first in 1979, the second in 1984 and the last in 2003.

Law No. 48/1979 provides specific regulation for access to the agent profession and registration in the register of agents; according to the new rule set by CAP, insurance agents will be registered in the section (a) of the Register of Insurance Intermediaries (see Article 109, paragraph 1 CAP).

In particular the law stipulates that both a single natural person and a company can be registered as agents.

400. The admission to the register is submitted to a number of requisites concerning the professional skills of the agent and the existence of honourable qualities. For registration of a company, these requirements are to be found in the person charged with the distribution (*delegato all'attività assicurativa*).

Following registration, a person or a company can exercise agency activity provided that they receive a written agreement from one or more insurance companies.[153]

401. National collective agreements (actually they all combine in the so-called ANA 2003) set the value of the indemnity in case of termination of the contract of agency and they prevail over individual agreements *in pejus* stipulated between the insurance company and the agent.

§4. The Liability of the Agent towards Clients and the Insurance Company

402. From the juridical point of view, the agent is an independent subject and he/she is not an employee of the insurance company. For this reason, the agent is directly liable towards the insurance company and/or the clients for the damages deriving from his/her activity. In the actual regime, the additional liability of the insurance company towards clients for damages caused by the agent has to be set in the light of the analysis of the specific activity realized by the agent.

The guidance rule has been until now that the insurance company has joint liability towards clients for damages resulting from the execution of the agent's activity in favour of the company; this solution has been elaborated by the courts in line with and application of the general principle of contract law that the principal is responsible for the acts of his/her auxiliaries within the scope of the agent's actual apparent authority or the execution of the conferred duties (Articles 1228 and 2049 CC).

403. Under the provisions of the new rules set by the *Codice delle Assicurazioni Private*, in particular Article 119 CAP, the solution mentioned above is confirmed because the insurance company is liable for damages deriving from the activity of the agents, even if those damages derive from frauds or other facts with criminal relevance.

404. In the actual system of law the duties of information of the agent are set by the general contract law. The *Codice delle Assicurazioni Private* increases those

---

153. See for details G. Volpe Putzolu, *Le assicurazioni. Produzione e distribuzione* (Bologna, 1992), in particular, 210ff.; D.Cerini, *Prodotti e servizi assicurativi. Distribuzione e intermediazione* (Milan, 2003), Ch. 1.

duties by obliging agents, as well as all other insurance intermediaries, to declare if they act under a duty to sell contract for one or more insurance company (Article 120 CAP).

In addition, agents are required to advise clients, on the basis of the information of given a product that fits their needs; an agent must describe the essential characteristics of the product offered and the obligations assumed by the insurance company according to the contract (Article 120, comma 3 CAP).

405. The Italian provision clearly overpasses the rule set by Article 3 of the directive and aims to introduce a general duty of *adeguatezza*.[154]

406. In addition to his/her liability towards the clients, the agent is liable towards the insurance company for any damage arising from his/her activity (liability in contract – Article 1228 CC).

In order to protect against unfaithful activities or damages from agents (especially in case of collection of premiums by the agent), insurance companies generally require a deposit or a guarantee bond at the time of the signing of the agency contract.

407. With the entry into force of the *Codice delle Assicurazioni Private*, all agents have to stipulate a liability insurance contract (Articles 111–112 CAP) for damages to clients as well as to the insurance company. The contract must have a minimum coverage of EUR 1 million per year and per accident and must be valid in all the European Union. ISVAP can periodically increase the level of coverage required according to the inflation rates.

---

154. For a wider analysis of the contract of agency see A. Baldassari, *Il contratto di agenzia*, Milan, coll. Il diritto privato oggi, 1992; R. Baldi & A. Venezia, *Il contratto di agenzia. La concessione di vendita. Il franchising*, 7th edn, (Milan, 2001); L. Casali, *L'agente e il broker di assicurazione* (Milan, 1993); Castellano & Menghi, Legge 7 febbraio 1979, No. 48. *Istituzione e funzionamento dell'albo nazionale degli agenti di assicurazione, Commentario*, in *Nuove leggi civili commentate* (1980), 1219ff.

Chapter 3. The Broker of Insurance and Reinsurance

§1. THE CONTRACT OF INSURANCE BROKERAGE

408. The second most important (and most ancient) figure of insurance interme-diary present on the Italian market is the *mediatore di assicurazione* or broker.

The contract of brokerage remained unnamed for a long period. In fact, before the creation of the national register of the brokers (due to the approval of Law No. 792/1984) the courts were pressed to find out the qualification of the contract of bro-kerage in order to set the applicable degree of liability in case of damage to clients and companies.

In order to describe the social function of the broker, and making reference to main contrast between his/her position and that of the agent considered a fiduciary person of the insurance company, the courts tried to apply the full set of rules con-cerning the contract of mediation, which is regulated Articles 1754 et seq. of the Civil Code.

409. Here mediation is defined as the 'activity of placing two or more parties in contact with the purpose of bringing about a transaction without being connected with either of such parties by way of collaboration or employment or representa-tion'. The relevant elements of the legal type of 'mediation' are consequently the independence of the broker from the two parties and the respect of good faith in the execution of his/her activity by the broker.

When making this process of interpretation, nonetheless, the courts arrived at the conclusion that the position of the broker and his/her eventual liability was to be found exclusively in the lack of result of the mediation activity, without any refer-ence to the assistance to the client and his/her need to be adequately advised.

410. It appeared quite soon, in any case, that the role of the broker went much further than the role of the typical mediator.

The definition of the broker as a pure mediator was consequently re-visited by the courts which, in perfect line with the customs already applied, considered the contract of insurance mediation or insurance brokerage an unnamed contract, where the professional skills and competence of the broker are offered to the clients who confer the mandate.

The existence of a special duty to assist the client was later affirmed by the law: in fact, when the Italian legislator gave implementation to the first Insurance Inter-mediary Directive (77/92/EEC) with the Law No. 792/1984, the complexity of the broker's activity was clearly affirmed. Article 1 of the said law identifies the insur-ance broker as follows:

> to the effects of the present law, the mediator of insurance and reinsurance is the one who professionally exercises the activity of *putting in contact* insur-ance companies or reinsurance companies – to which he is not linked by any commitments – subjects that intend to cover risks with his cooperation, *help-ing* them in the determination of the content of the contract and *eventually cooperating* in the management of the said contracts.

411. It is quite clear that the aim of the quoted definition was to identify the position of the broker in order to restrict the duty of registration to the public register. Nevertheless, the definition contained in Article 1 of the Law 792/1984 gave the basis for the distinction of three different components of the insurance broker's activity: (1) the activity of mediation, which follows the rules of Articles 1754 et seq. of the Civil Code; (2) the activity of assistance in favour of the client, with the important effect that from now on this duty of consultancy and assistance is to be considered a legal one as it arises from the law and it cannot be derogated by the parties; and (3) the eventual activity of administration of the contract. This identification has an important role in order to determine the eventual professional liability of the broker.[155]

412. It is important to consider that Article 109, paragraph 2 of *Codice delle Assicurazioni Private* expressly mentions insurance intermediaries by providing a (partially) different definition: in fact the new rule defines as brokers those who act for the client and in the absence of the power to represent the insurance company.

The new regulation does not mention the activity of management of the intermediated contracts by the broker which nevertheless can always be assumed by the broker as per the effect of a specific agreement with the client.

§2. THE RESPONSIBILITY OF THE BROKER

413. As seen, the position of the broker is quite peculiar in the intermediary scene because his/her activity is in fact more that of assistance of the prospective policyholder and insured rather than that of mere mediation between two parties. In addition he/she can execute other material activities in the eventual exercise of the duty of cooperation which has to be specifically assumed by contract. In other words, in the eyes of the legislator the broker loses his/her neutral role in order to become a sort of auxiliary of the prospective insured.

This position is strengthened by the fact that the law (Article 1 L.792/1984, new rule Article 109, paragraph 2 of CAP) requires the broker to be independent from insurance companies so that he/she cannot have the authority to accept proposals for insurance nor can he/she assume any power to represent or bind in any way the insurer.

On the other hand the insurance broker can represent the prospective policyholder in order to negotiate with several insurance companies on his/her behalf to obtain the best possible insurance coverage on the market and with reference to the special needs of the client.

414. The responsibility of the broker is consequently a complex one and the standard of care required as well as the regime of liability have to be determined according to the cause of the damage and the type of activity in question.

---

155. In fact the existence of a 'duty of *adeguatezza*' was set also in the pre-existing regulation by ISVAP (Circular Letter 553/D/2004 and Circular Letter 551/D/2005) which will be abrogated with the entry into force of the Code and additional rules to be approved under Art. 355 CAP.

Those standards are consequently to be found both in the general rules concerning the mediation contract (Article 1754 CC) as far as the activity of putting into contact the two parties is concerned, while the applicable regime of liability will differ if the damage arises from the execution of a different duty assumed by the broker or existing by law, i.e., while the liability of mediators is a strict one, the liability of the broker for damages deriving from a lack of consultancy and assistance is based on the general rule of Article 2222 CC, which regulates the liability for professional activities by imposing a rule of negligence.

415. It is worth remembering that the courts have quite often declared the liability of insurance brokers for lack of assistance and advice in case of the transfer of the insured position from one insurance contract to the other when the transfer gave place to a lack of coverage.[156]

Finally, when judging the eventual responsibility of the broker for material activities or management of the insurance contract in favour of the client (i.e., payment of the premium, transfer of information or communication) the broker's liability is set according to principles of strict liability.

416. The broker is also liable towards the insurance company for any damage arising from his/her activity. A tort liability is in this case applied.

417. The law poses various economic protections for insured parties and undertakings towards damages deriving from the activity of the brokers. In fact, Law No. 792/1984 provides that all brokers (both private persons and broker companies) should have a liability insurance for damages towards insurance companies and clients. The coverage and economic limits of the policy are set by the law itself (Article 5, Law No. 792/1984) and will have to be adjusted according to the new law (Article 110 CAP). The law also requires brokers to adhere to a guarantee fund which assure economic recovery in cases where the professional liability coverage does not operare (i.e., in case of fraud of the broker – Article 4 of Law No. 792/1984).

418. The new rules confirm the duties of the brokers to have a minimum financial capacity (Article 112), to stipulate a professional indemnity insurance (as provided by Article 110 CAP) and to contribute to the guarantee fund (Article 115 CAP) in addition to the general duty to set up a separate and segregated account (Article 117 CAP) and the already mentioned rule of effectiveness of payment set by Article 118, second comma CAP.

§3. PAYMENT OF THE BROKER

419. According to the use of the market, the broker is paid by the insurance company and not by the insured, or even better the full payment for the intermediation activity comes from the company. This result, which does not practically change the

---

156. See below, para. 329ff.

charge of the payment as it is finally supported by the insured, who fully pays the premium, here including the commission, has been considered legitimate and correct by the courts.[157]

This use is confirmed by the 'Letter of Intent' between ANIA – AIBA – FIBRAS, which is a gentlemen's agreement signed between the professional association of insurances (ANIA) and the two major associations of Italian brokers (AIBA and FIBRAS). The Letter of Intent is also an important reference because it is binding for the associates and it is an informal reference for judges.

---

157. Corte App. Bologna, 18 Jul. 1992, FI, 1993, I, 577 with reference to the transfer from a contract based on the 'loss occurrence' system of coverage to a 'claims made' system where the result was a temporary lack of coverage for the insured.

Chapter 4. Sub-agents and Free Producers

420.   Until the approval of *Codice delle Assicurazioni Private*, sub-agents did not receive much attention from the legislator. The activity of sub-agents consequently developed in the context of general contract law and in particular the rules governing the agency contract were applied to the relation between the agent and the sub-agent, making an exception of the power of representation, as their position can be described as a 'sub-contract' of the agency scheme.

This is to be overruled by the entry into force of the *Codice delle Assicurazioni Private*. First of all, under the new regulation sub-agents must be registered under section (e) of the Register of Insurance Intermediaries. In addition, they have to respect the duty of information established by Article 120 CAP.

421.   As per the effect of the *Codice delle Assicurazioni Private* all subjects who pursue activities of insurance mediation, here including preliminary activities of presentation of products of have to be registered either under section (c) direct producers for insurance companies, or under section (e) if they operate for another insurance intermediary.

This represents a fundamental change as the activity of so-called free producers was completely non-regulated by Italian legislation. In fact, the activity of such persons had to be built, so to say, from a negative perspective, that is to say that their role was not specifically considered by the law but they only had to operate without invading the roles of agents and brokers, i.e., they could not give consultancy and could not act in the name of the insurer.

422.   As anticipated, the presence of free producers is now to be read in the light of the implementation of the second Directive on Insurance Intermediaries. In particular, according to Article 109 paragraph 2, non-occasional free producers have to be registered in section (e) of the Register of Insurance Intermediaries and to satisfy the specific requirements for the inscriptions provided by Article 111 (professional and honourable requirements).

Chapter 5. Insurance Distribution by Means of Networks Based on Multilevel Marketing, Network Marketing and Similar Marketing Techniques

423. The distribution of insurance through a multilevel network or network marketing is not really developed in the Italian market. It is in fact the presence of foreign companies where these types of distribution techniques are well known that has contributed to the spread into the insurance distribution sector of multilevel and network marketing strategies originated in other commercial sectors.

The general characteristics of such distribution techniques are to be outlined by the market and are not set by legislative forms.

In fact, these kinds of distribution networks are characterized by the presence of at least the following elements: (a) the presence of a number of distributors not provided with a company mandate and consequently operating under the control of other intermediaries at the upper level of the distribution chain; (b) the activity of the same distributors outside the agency, the latter having an exclusively or prevalently indirect underwriting activity; (c) the site of the activity of such distributors is the territory where they work directly in contact with potential policy-holders; (d) the multiplying number of levels of the chain considering that each distributor can acquire other subjects who will be under his/her supervision and for the production of which he/she receives a part of the commission.

424. The insurance world would not take into special account such forms of distribution, which are in principle fully legitimate and within the freedom of organizing the distribution chain of all economic operators, if not for the fact that multilevel distribution has originated in the product market and not in the service one, especially that of insurance. This is a commercial sector where not only the mere acceptance on the part of the consumer is necessary to close the bargain, but that also requires (both before and after the underwriting of a policy) the assistance of a competent operator to ensure a full understanding of the contract provisions, to manage the ensuing guarantees and to comply with the requirements envisaged in the case of a claim for insurance benefits.

425. Once the multilevel and network systems of distribution made their appearance in the Italian market in the middle of the 1990s, ISVAP promptly required some fundamental elements to be respected in order to protect the consumers (Circular Letter 487/D/2000). For some years, ISVAP circular letter was the source regulating the multilevel marketing in insurance. It should be noted that many of the requirements set out by the Circular Letter 487/D/2000 have anticipated those of Title IX of the *Codice delle Assicurazioni Private* in application of the second Directive on Insurance Intermediaries.

The Code in fact only provides that Consumer protection is built on specific requirements to be respected by the insurance company itself as well as by the involved intermediaries.

426. In the first place, the control authority insists on the need for supervision of each level of the distribution chain. For this reason, it is necessary to issue an agency mandate to the party who individually or by means of a company coordinates the aforementioned network of distributors.

Companies will be obliged to define or integrate this mandate and the related administrative specifications, bearing in mind the operational characteristics of these sales techniques that – giving rise to a production that is not directly attributable to the professional agent, but almost exclusively to his/her external collaborators – require the implementation of suitable controls at every level.

To this end, undertakings are required to establish a system of control over single auxiliaries and, in particular, to ensure the professional competence of each single person involved in the distribution process.

427. The size of the network, its presence in one or more provinces or regions or over the whole national territory and the extension of the underwritten portfolio will represent the first operational reference parameters to assess the efficiency and speed of the agency's monitoring activity.

Special attention is given to the support of each network component by the agent. The agency itself must support to individual canvassers, constantly monitoring their activity, immediately identifying any operational disorders, satisfying requests from potential policyholders for more detailed pre-contractual information and further implementing the working procedures described below.

428. At the same time, undertakings are required, as far as their responsibility goes, to put in place adequate internal control procedures, and to reach a prior agreement with the agency heading the multilevel network in relation to the types of product to be distributed by means of the described network, the definition of connected underwriting procedures, the timing for reporting of acquired sales, the carrying out of controls and inspections at least every three months in the areas defined below and, in general, on the overall activity involved.

429. On the basis of this dual responsibility, the control authority has set out some specific guidelines towards ensuring consumer protection by limiting the use of multilevel techniques by specific subjects or with reference to specific products.

430. In particular, the multilevel and similar techniques cannot be used for the distribution of unit-linked life insurance products or for the offering of services under Article 9*ter* of the Legislative Decree No. 124/1995 (individual pension plans). The selling of these kinds of products is reserved to professional intermediaries (agents and brokers) acting directly.

431. Multilevel or network marketing techniques cannot be used by the insurance broker registered under section b) of Article 109 of the CAP: in fact, in the broker-client relation there is a fiduciary side that would obviously be frustrated by the activity of these canvassers, with all the consequences deriving from the avoidance of the splitting of activity as envisaged by Article 2 (I paragraph) of the above-mentioned law, the non-applicability of the professional liability policy (intermediaries may only explicitly guarantee the activities of the broker's employees and not of any external canvassers), and the difficulty of contemplating the involvement of the guarantee fund as envisaged by Article 4 (I paragraph, letter (f) of the above-mentioned law).

432. For similar reasons, EU undertakings that have been licensed to enter the Italian market under the freedom of services (for whom there is a legal prohibition to operate in the host country by means of a stable organization) cannot use a network or multilevel chain.

Chapter 6. Cross-selling and Interaction between Insurance Companies and Banks

§1. INTRODUCTION

433. The actual economic trend shows a deep interaction between insurance companies and banking institutions.

The fields of integration and cooperation, as well as those of competition, are in fact quite varied. They relate to the creation and structuring of products, they relate to the acquisition of crossed shareholdings and they also relate to the distribution process.

§2. DISTRIBUTION OF INSURANCE THROUGH BANKS: THE ITALIAN MODEL OF BANCASSURANCE

434. Banks are the main competitors of traditional intermediaries (agents and brokers) in the distribution of insurance, especially with reference to life insurance contracts.

Nonetheless, the distribution of insurance by banks has been strongly contrasted by other intermediaries, especially by the agents, and a legal discipline is still lacking, as the only references we have are administrative rules set by the ISVAP after a long period of discussion and pronunciation by the criminal courts, and the Ministry of Industry, now partially reproduced in the Code of Private Insurances.

435. In practical terms, the bank insurance model can be realized in different ways:

(a) The bank can bring in independent brokers who will be in charge of the distribution process.
(b) Another solution is the stipulation of group insurance contracts whereby the bank is the contracting party for the benefit of the clients. This model realizes in fact a sort of *fictio* which appears evident especially when the bank has no interest in the insurance contract if not the payment of a commission (which is in fact typical of the distribution sector). This model of group insurance applies the scheme of contract on behalf of third parties defined by Article 1891 CC. In this scheme, the contractor is the agent of the insured and no correction to the general principles of law is provided in order to better protect the position of individual insured parties.
(c) Most recently, an independent and autonomous role of intermediary has been recognized to bank institutions. The activity of the bank as intermediary is to be built according to some specific limits set by the ISVAP Circular Letter No. 241 of 1995 (and now reproduced in Title IX of *Codice delle Assicurazioni Private*).

The main aspect of Circular Letter No. 241/1995 is that the role of the bank is that of a mere executor of the insurer: it does not have any power to represent the insurer (this distinguishes the bank from the insurance agent) nor can the bank give any consultancy to the client (in this sense it is different from the broker).

Under the provision of the Code of Private Insurance banks can be registered under section (d) of the *Registro degli Intermediari* (Article 109 CAP). In principle, they could also be registered under any other section of the Register if they satisfy the necessary requirements.

436. According to Circular Letter No. 241/1995 a bank could sell only standardized insurance products (*prodotti standardizzati*). That means that the product cannot be modified by the bank operator who can only chose between the general and particular clauses already set by the insurer. The rule is reproduced in Article 119, paragraph 2 CAP. This limitation does not apply if the bank is registered under a section other than (d) of the Register of Insurance Intermediaries, i.e., if the bank obtains the registration as agent under letter (a) of the same register, provided it respects all necessary requirements.

437. In fact, the most successful products for bank insurance have been life insurance products, mostly investment products. In recent years, other kinds of products have also been distributed, e.g., automobile insurance.

A developing market is that of products to supplement mortgages (especially consumer credit insurance). In this case, the borrower takes out a cash-value life or indemnity policy that is sufficient to cover the price of the home or other good plus a little extra. At the end of the policy's term or in the event of death, the loan is paid off.

§3. The Distribution of Bank Products by Insurance Companies and their Agents

438. The Communication of the Bank of Italy of 26 February 1999 has allowed banks to sell their products through auxiliaries outside bank offices. In particular, the sale of bank products is allowed to insurance companies through their agents.

The position of agents selling bank products is similar to that of banks selling insurance products. Agents can offer only standardized bank contracts and cannot provide by analysis rating activities. In other words, insurance agents pay their access to the bank sales by reducing the activities they can offer, in a way that is quite similar to the sale of insurance products by the banks.

Chapter 7. The Role of Investment Companies or SIM

439. Investment companies (*Società di Intermediazione Mobiliare* or SIM) are subject to the provisions of the Legislative Decree No. 58 of 24 February 1998, also called *Testo Unico sulla Intermediazione Finanziaria* (or TUF).

440. Investment companies (as well as banks) exercise their activity either in their office or outside (*fuori sede*) in cooperation with financial promoters (*promotori finanziari*) who are enrolled within the National Register kept by CONSOB (the control authority for companies and the stock market).

Investment companies are authorized to sell insurance products and services by *Testo Unico Intermediazione Finanziaria*.

441. The limits of their activity in the offering of insurance products can be traced by way of analogy with that of banks. The alternative is that a representative of the investment company obtains registration on the agent register established by Law No. 48/1979 (new rule section (a) of the Register set by Article 109 CAP) and is consequently responsible for the distribution activity realized by the SIM.

It should be considered that, after the approval of the Code of Private Insurances, SIMs can register under section (d) of the Register of Insurance Intermediaries, provided that they do not register under any other section, if they possess the necessary requirements.

Chapter 8. The Distance Selling of Insurance Products

§1. The Need for Special Regulation for Distance Selling of Financial Products

442. Given the growing interest shown by undertakers and consumers in the use of the Internet and other forms of distance selling for the supply and purchase of insurance products, ISVAP has deemed it necessary to give a first reference framework for operations through the Internet aimed at reconciling the technological developments of the net with the current regulations on insurance business, for the primary purpose of ensuring adequate consumer protection.

The relevant discipline is actually set by ISVAP Regulation no.34 of 2010. In many ways, it reproduces the Circular Letter No. 393/D/of 17 January 1999[158] which anticipated many of the provisions set by Directive EC/2002/65. In fact, the approval of *Codice delle Assicurazioni Private* has not implemented the Directive on Distance Selling of financial services except in a very general rule concerning pre-contractual information set out in Article 121 CAP which will be described below.

I. The Identification of the Operating Subjects

443. The first fundamental step is considered the setting of procedures of internal control in order to assure that the company keeps control over the subjects who distribute her products using distance selling techniques. First of all, it must be said that the use of the Internet by insurance companies as a channel for the direct sale of products implies that the company takes on full responsibility in advance for the activity exercised by those actually charged with the management of the website and/or to the interaction through the e-mail.

444. Given that distance selling techniques and in particular Internet offerings have only recently been applied to the insurance sector with very delicate implications, ISVAP requires each authorized company to adopt adequate internal control procedures. The goal of these procedures is to allow the *a posteriori* reconstruction of the terms, times and characteristics of the interactions undertaken by competent staff.

445. Insurance companies have to make periodical and systematic controls – for example on a sample basis – on the completeness and regularity of the communications and documents (information brochures, proposals, policies, receipts, certificates, marks, etc.) actually received by the policyholder.

At any rate the insurance companies must see that all the initiatives taken for the distribution of their products through the Internet – either directly or through the

---

158. Cass. 21 Dec. 1988 No. 5183, in GC, Mass., 1988.

intermediation of independent agencies – envisage adequate terms of premium payment capable of guaranteeing the highest possible degree of certainty, security and confidentiality of the payments made by policyholders.

446. The second fundamental step is the identification of the undertaking and verification of its license to pursue insurance activity in Italy. This is ensured thanks to a precondition for the protection of future policyholders. The way in which the undertaking describes itself on the Internet must make it easily possible to identify the undertaking and verify whether it is licensed to pursue insurance business in Italy.

In this regard, as far as authorized undertakings are concerned, the website must indicate all the elements necessary to identify the company (i.e., the name, the address of the undertaking's head office). In particular, the information on the date when the authorization was issued, the date and number of the Italian Official Journal in which the deed was published as well as the mention that the company is subject to ISVAP's supervision have to be accessible on the Internet.

447. As to licensed undertakings (either on a free provision of services basis or under the right of establishment) the site must indicate the company's registered name, the address of its head office and, if this is the case, of the branch which concludes the contracts (including the telephone and fax numbers), the declaration that it is authorized to pursue insurance business in Italy and the mention of the supervisory authority of the home country and of ISVAP, as supervisory authority of the host country.

Moreover, undertakings licensed to carry on business by way of free provision of services must indicate the name of the fiscal representative as well as of the representative for the handling of claims.

II. Information for Policyholders Prior to the Conclusion of the Contract

448. As is well known, Italian and foreign insurance undertakings carrying on business on the territory of the Italian Republic must meet the obligation to communicate information to policyholders before concluding the contract. The complete Information Dossier, for both life and non-life insurance contracts, has to be fully published in the website of the company, as well as for products sold with traditional techniques.

449. Therefore, in addition to the general rules, when selling products through the Internet, some further conditions must be satisfied.

The information brochure and contract terms must be available for reference on the company's website, adequately revised to take present provisions into account.

450. The file containing the text of the information brochure must in no way be modifiable by the user. Alternatively, the information brochure must be sent to the policyholder, before concluding the contract, by using transmission techniques which allow the reception of the document on paper or on any other durable medium available to and accessible by the policyholder. It can be clarified that by 'durable medium' is meant any instrument allowing the policyholder to store information addressed to him/her personally (such as floppy discs, CD-ROMs or a hard drive on which e-mail is stored, etc.).

The mere possibility of the policyholder printing the information brochure available on the site is not considered sufficient to fulfil the obligation to provide information, since the brochure must be personally and specifically sent to the policyholder.

451. In this regard the obligation to provide information is also considered to be fulfilled when the system is conceived in such a way that the pre-contractual negotiations cannot continue if the policyholder has not stored the information brochure on a durable medium beforehand.

452. Undertakings should also turn their attention to the need to ensure that, in the case of changes or updating of the texts, the information available on the site corresponds exactly to that which is actually sent to the policyholder.

If the undertaking, in compliance with the above-mentioned provisions, chooses to transmit the information brochure in an electronic format, it will be the undertaking's concern to guarantee the correspondence between the text of the information brochure available on the site and that actually sent to the policyholder (for instance by depositing the original on paper with a notary). These rules, set by Regulation, are confirmed by Article 121 CAP.

§2. The Special Need for Certainty About the Time when the Contract is Concluded and Insurance Cover Becomes Effective

453. Without prejudice to the current legal provisions on the conclusion of the contract (the proposal that meets the acceptance as per Article 1326 of the Civil Code or the supply to the public under Article 1336 of the Civil Code), the information brochure and the policy conditions must indicate the means of concluding the contract and clearly specify the moment when the contract is concluded and, if different, the time when the insurance coverage becomes effective.

The exact definition of the time when the contract is concluded is in fact fundamental for determining when exactly the delay for terminating the contract starts from, while the determination of the exact time when the insurance coverage becomes effective is essential in order to prevent any litigation in case of claims.

454. To avoid any uncertainly, neither the time when the contract is concluded nor when the cover becomes effective must be established with reference to elements that the policyholder does not and cannot know (such as, for instance, the date when the undertaking receives the cheque for the payment of the premium or the time when the undertaking is informed that the premium has been credited on its current account, etc.).

455. With regard to motor vehicle liability contracts the policyholder must also be able to immediately obtain the insurance certificate and mark on paper. While waiting for these documents to be sent, the policyholder must immediately be given – by fax or by any other adequate means – a receipt of payment of the premium to be shown on the vehicle, as required by Italian legislation.

§3. SUBSEQUENT MANAGEMENT OF THE CONTRACT

456. Given that policyholders must also be guaranteed adequate assistance after the conclusion of the contract, the brochure must provide information on how the contract is managed, with regard for example to the means of paying the subsequent premiums, of reporting claims, of applying for surrenders, loans, claims settlements, etc. For motor vehicle liability insurance the policyholder must also be informed of the terms for obtaining the motor third-party liability risk certificate at least three days before the expiry date of the contract. Needless to say the policyholder must be able to get the certificate at no extra charge.

457. As for life assurance, the brochure must also indicate how the undertaking intends to provide information during the term of the contract.

458. At any rate the undertaking's structural organization should be able to provide the benefits insured under the contracts concluded through the Internet. With reference to motor vehicle liability insurance, the web page should mention the competent claims settlement departments or any other similar structure. In this regard the information brochure should contain a cross reference to this indication.

§4. RIGHT OF CANCELLATION

459. In case of supply of insurance contracts with distance selling techniques, the insured can cancel the contract as provided by Article 177 CAP. In order to ensure the possibility of exercising such a fundamental right, the information brochure must clearly state the first day on which it is possible to exercise it and the procedures to follow.

Under the above regulation, the undertaking, within thirty days of receiving the notification of cancellation, must reimburse the policyholder any paid-up premiums net of the portion relating to the period for which the contract was effective and of any costs incurred for issuing it, provided that the costs were determined and quantified according to Article 177 CAP).

460. In accordance with Article 176 CAP, the right of cancellation must also apply to a proposal for a policy. It must in fact be possible to cancel the contract before it is actually concluded.

461. One should remember that, with the implementation of EC directive on distance selling, the right of cancellation is provided for all life and non-life insurance contracts. The importance of this right is confirmed by the fact that, even prior to the legal duty to provide for the right of withdrawal, Circular Letter 393/D/1999 had already suggested the opportunity to apply such a right for all plocies. Finally a general right of cancellation for all contracts sold by distance selling techniques is now provided by D. Lgs. 190/2005.

§5. Law Applicable to the Contract and Competent Judicial Authority

462. Given that the law envisages an obligation to inform the policyholder of the law applicable to the contract, the information brochure should also draw the policyholder's attention to the fact that, if the law chosen is the law of another country, in case of litigation the contract will be governed by the law of that other country.

463. Moreover, if according to national and international regulations on competent jurisdiction the judicial authority competent for settling controversies can be different from the Italian one, this must be clearly stated in the information brochure.

§6. Requirement for a Written Form

464. Under recent regulations (Article 15 of Law 59/97, Presidential Decree No. 513 of 10 November 1997, Decree of the President of the Council of Ministers of 8 February 1999), a telematic document underwritten with a digital signature, regardless of the subject that has made it, satisfies the requirement of the written form and is considered as probative evidence like any private deed as per Article 2702 of the Civil Code.

Therefore, when the digital signature comes fully into effect, the documents underwritten by using this kind of signature will replace documents on paper for all legal purposes.

465. Pending the implementation of this provision, the written form is still required, as well as the signature and the mailing of certain documents and statements by ordinary means. The most important are:

– the insurance policy, including policy conditions and contract terms as per Article 1341 of the Civil Code, as well as any other document to be underwritten by the insurer (Article 1888 of the Civil Code);
– the statements made by the policyholder under Articles 1892–1893 of the Civil Code on the risk to be insured;
– the consent of the third party on whose life the contract is concluded (Article 1919 of the Civil Code);
– the policyholder's statement that before concluding the contract he/she has been given the information brochure on paper or on another durable medium.

When drawing up policy conditions, the company is required to leave out terms that may be regarded as unfair under Directive 93/13/EEC, which have been transposed in the Code of Consumers.

§7. SPECIFIC REQUIREMENTS CONCERNING MONEY LAUNDERING

466. Regulation 34/2010 also considers the specific problem of money laundering with reference to distance selling.

ISVAP consequently considers that due to the distance the use of the Internet makes it more difficult for the undertaking or its representatives to identify the person that makes or receives payments exceeding 20 million lire or takes out a life policy or else, if this is the case, his/her proxy (Article 4.1 of ministerial decree of 19 December 1991 reads 'data on the opening of accounts, deposits or other permanent relations must be gathered in the presence of the holder or of his or her proxy … ').

467. In this regard we refer to the application criteria of the ministerial decree established by the Ministry of the Treasury (Communication of 5 June 1992), which, if direct identification is not possible, require the intermediary concerned (in this case the insurance undertaking) to obtain a declaration issued by another intermediary as per Law No. 197/91 who has already identified this person in the performance of his/her activity.

§8. DISTANCE SELLING BY INSURANCE AGENTS

468. With regard to insurance agents, from a logical and legal point of view the use of the Internet as a sale channel rests both on the mandate given by the company (provided that the latter has satisfied all the conditions for the taking up of business on the Italian market) and on registration with his/her national professional order.

The sale through the Internet by EU agents – if directed to Italian consumers – falls within the wider scope of the free provision of services, and therefore requires as a precondition that the agent be registered with his/her national professional order as laid down in existing legislation after the implementation of EC Directive 2002/92.

469. The Italian control authority insists that insurance undertakings licensed to carry on business by way of free provision of services are forbidden to give any kind of agencies to persons established on the territory of provision of services.

470. The Circular Letter also identifies specific requirements that must be observed if insurance intermediaries decide to operate through the Internet with actual or prospective clients. One should consider that some of these requirements may appear particularly severe and will have to be revised when the Directive on Distance selling is implemented in Italy.

In particular, given some delicate aspects connected to the use of the Internet, and considering that companies are required to supervise their sales network, ISVAP provides as follows:

- the agents concerned must have previously sent a written notification to their mandators (the insurance companies) about the use of this instrument of distance selling. This notification must indicate the terms and object of the selling, as well as the commitment to comply with the instructions given by this circular letter and to notify the company of any future change in its procedures;
- agents must establish the above-mentioned procedures together with their mandators and are at any rate subject to subsequent verification by the company over the actual use of this sales instrument, for the purpose of preventing any misuse and abuse;
- agents shall take on any responsibility *vis-à-vis* their mandators – also in case of *culpa in eligendo* or *in vigilando* relating to the activity of their subordinate staff – arising out of the performance of their tasks by means of distance selling;
- when creating a website or sending e-mails – also as a first approach with the potential client – agents can never leave out the express indication of the data about their registration with the national professional order (registration number and date) and with the Chamber of Commerce, Industry, Handicrafts and Agriculture, the address of their offices, their telephone and fax numbers, the administrative code that they have been assigned by their mandators (the complete registered name and head office of the latter must also be indicated);
- more specifically, in case of multi-agencies, it must be made clear which of the above-mentioned mandators guarantees the product offered;
- if the agent is an undertaking, the mention of registration with the agents' national order must mention the lawyer or the legal representative of the company, or any other person having the necessary powers and charged by the company to perform the activity of insurance agent;
- regardless of who takes on the initiative of the contract, be it the agent or the policyholder, the direct interaction through the electronic mail must subsequently be reserved to the person registered with the national professional order of insurance agents, on pain of breach of Law 48/79 (new rule Title IX CAP), or to one or more of his/her proxies, but it can never be entrusted to autonomous collaborators (sub-agents, canvassers, dealers and other external staff).

§9. DISTANCE SELLING AND INSURANCE BROKERS

471. For insurance and reinsurance brokers the problems raised by the use of the worldwide web are somewhat different, given that under Article 109 CAP the broker cannot accept any commitment toward insurance companies and therefore cannot conclude contracts on their behalf, on pain of losing his/her capacity as broker recognized by the law.

472. The use of the Internet by EU insurance brokers – if directed to Italian consumers (under the terms described below) – falls within the wider scope of free provision of services. Undertakings licensed to operate on a free provision of services basis can start up dealings with insurance brokers established in Italy given that the law does not provide for any restrictions on such companies.

Having said this the broker is free to create a site through which he/she can advertise his/her services as an independent intermediary and possibly obtain a mandate by the policyholder, as is the usual procedure, as well as to use the resources of the Internet (e.g., the e-mail) to present proposals for cover to his/her client. Finally, the broker will avail himself/herself of the said resources in order to act as a go-between with the companies, and use his/her site and/or his/her e-mail as a 'bridge' and 'filter' between the two parties in the potential insurance relationship.

If the broker issues formal cover notes to the client, these can have effect for the company and the client only if they show the essential data on the acceptance of the risk by the insurance company. Otherwise these notes will be binding only for the broker and the client, without having any effect for the company. The broker must clearly specify this circumstance to the addressee of the cover note.

473. In compliance with the provisions on the regular circulation of vehicles and craft, the insurance undertaking using distance selling techniques shall, as evidence for third parties that the risk relating to motor vehicle liability has been covered, issue in due time the documents required by the Code of Private Insurances).

Chapter 9. Litigation in Insurance

474. Insurance matters are often litigated in courts. In recent years, two important new disciplines have been introduced in Italian civil procedure law and they impact directly on insurance litigation: the new rules on class action, on one side, and the introduction of compulsory mediation for insurance controversies.

§1. CLASS ACTION

475. The debate over the introduction of class actions in Italy is old enough to have recalled a lot of comments. Nevertheless, if we leave apart the action for injunction as described under Article 37 of the Consumer Code – which provides for a 'collective' moment in the development of the case and has been used in several cases concerning insurance contracts-general class actions are not yet a reality in our legal system.

476. Of course, consumer associations can assist the filing claims on behalf of a single or groups of consumers to obtain judicial orders against corporations that cause injury or damage to consumers. Indeed, these types of claims were increasing and Italian courts have recently allowed them against banks that continue to apply compound interest on retail clients' current account overdrafts. On these bases, the introduction of class actions was assumed on the new government's agenda. In 2004, the Italian parliament considered the introduction of a type of class action lawsuit, specifically in the area of consumers' law, but only at the end of 2007 the Senato della Repubblica with the financial law for 2008 (a financial document of the government for the economic management of the national budget), introduced Article 140*bis* of the Italian consumers' code. This new rule regulates the class action ('azione collettiva risarcitoria'). Nevertheless, this rule has had a long and difficult life so far. In fact, it should have entered into force on 1 January 2008 but its effectiveness has been postponed by the Government for three times: on 29 June 2008, on 1 January 2009, on 29 June 2009, finally on July 2009, by way of Article 49 of law n. 99/2009: this last time, Article 140*bis* has been completely rewritten:[159] the new rules are applicable since 1 January 2010. Since then, a number of

---

159. Actual text of Art. 140*bis* of the consumer code "Art. 140*bis*. – *(Azione di classe)*. – *1*. I diritti individuali omogenei dei consumatori e degli utenti di cui al comma 2 sono tutelabili anche attraverso l'azione di classe, secondo le previsioni del presente articolo. A tal fine ciascun componente della classe, anche mediante associazioni cui dà mandato o comitati cui partecipa, può agire per l'accertamento della responsabilità e per la condanna al risarcimento del danno e alle restituzioni.

    2.   L'azione tutela:
        a)   i diritti contrattuali di una pluralità di consumatori e utenti che versano nei confronti di una stessa impresa in situazione identica, inclusi i diritti relativi a contratti stipulati ai sensi degli articoli 1341 e 1342 del codice civile;
        b)   i diritti identici spettanti ai consumatori finali di un determinato prodotto nei confronti del relativo produttore, anche a prescindere da un diretto rapporto contrattuale;

    c)   i diritti identici al ristoro del pregiudizio derivante agli stessi consumatori e utenti da pratiche commerciali scorrette o da comportamenti anticoncorrenziali.

3.   I consumatori e utenti che intendono avvalersi della tutela di cui al presente articolo aderiscono all'azione di classe, senza ministero di difensore. L'adesione comporta rinuncia a ogni azione restitutoria o risarcitoria individuale fondata sul medesimo titolo, salvo quanto previsto dal comma 15. L'atto di adesione, contenente, oltre all'elezione di domicilio, l'indicazione degli elementi costitutivi del diritto fatto valere con la relativa documentazione probatoria, è depositato in cancelleria, anche tramite l'attore, nel termine di cui al comma 9, lettera b). Gli effetti sulla prescrizione ai sensi degli articoli 2943 e 2945 del codice civile decorrono dalla notificazione della domanda e, per coloro che hanno aderito successivamente, dal deposito dell'atto di adesione.

4.   La domanda è proposta al tribunale ordinario avente sede nel capoluogo della regione in cui ha sede l'impresa, ma per la Valle d'Aosta è competente il tribunale di Torino, per il Trentino-Alto Adige e il Friuli-Venezia Giulia è competente il tribunale di Venezia, per le Marche, l'Umbria, l'Abruzzo e il Molise è competente il tribunale di Roma e per la Basilicata e la Calabria è competente il tribunale di Napoli. Il tribunale tratta la causa in composizione collegiale.

5.   La domanda si propone con atto di citazione notificato anche all'ufficio del pubblico ministero presso il tribunale adìto, il quale può intervenire limitatamente al giudizio di ammissibilità.

6.   All'esito della prima udienza il tribunale decide con ordinanza sull'ammissibilità della domanda, ma può sospendere il giudizio quando sui fatti rilevanti ai fini del decidere è in corso un'istruttoria davanti a un'autorità indipendente ovvero un giudizio davanti al giudice amministrativo. La domanda è dichiarata inammissibile quando è manifestamente infondata, quando sussiste un conflitto di interessi ovvero quando il giudice non ravvisa l'identità dei diritti individuali tutelabili ai sensi del comma 2, nonchè quando il proponente non appare in grado di curare adeguatamente l'interesse della classe.

7.   L'ordinanza che decide sulla ammissibilità è reclamabile davanti alla corte d'appello nel termine perentorio di trenta giorni dalla sua comunicazione o notificazione se anteriore. Sul reclamo la corte d'appello decide con ordinanza in camera di consiglio non oltre quaranta giorni dal deposito del ricorso. Il reclamo dell'ordinanza ammissiva non sospende il procedimento davanti al tribunale.

8.   Con l'ordinanza di inammissibilità, il giudice regola le spese, anche ai sensi dell'articolo 96 del codice di procedura civile, e ordina la più opportuna pubblicità a cura e spese del soccombente.

9.   Con l'ordinanza con cui ammette l'azione il tribunale fissa termini e modalità della più opportuna pubblicità, ai fini della tempestiva adesione degli appartenenti alla classe. L'esecuzione della pubblicità è condizione di procedibilità della domanda. Con la stessa ordinanza il tribunale:

    a)   definisce i caratteri dei diritti individuali oggetto del giudizio, specificando i criteri in base ai quali i soggetti che chiedono di aderire sono inclusi nella classe o devono ritenersi esclusi dall'azione;

    b)   fissa un termine perentorio, non superiore a centoventi giorni dalla scadenza di quello per l'esecuzione della pubblicità, entro il quale gli atti di adesione, anche a mezzo dell'attore, sono depositati in cancelleria. Copia dell'ordinanza è trasmessa, a cura della cancelleria, al Ministero dello sviluppo economico che ne cura ulteriori forme di pubblicità, anche mediante la pubblicazione sul relativo sito *internet*.

10.   È escluso l'intervento di terzi ai sensi dell'articolo 105 del codice di procedura civile.

11.   Con l'ordinanza con cui ammette l'azione il tribunale determina altresì il corso della procedura assicurando, nel rispetto del contraddittorio, l'equa, efficace e sollecita gestione del processo. Con la stessa o con successiva ordinanza, modificabile o revocabile in ogni tempo, il tribunale prescrive le misure atte a evitare indebite ripetizioni o complicazioni nella presentazione di prove o argomenti; onera le parti della pubblicità ritenuta necessaria a tutela degli aderenti; regola nel modo che ritiene più opportuno l'istruzione probatoria e disciplina ogni altra questione di rito, omessa ogni formalità non essenziale al contraddittorio.

12.   Se accoglie la domanda, il tribunale pronuncia sentenza di condanna con cui liquida, ai sensi dell'articolo 1226 del codice civile, le somme definitive dovute a coloro che hanno aderito all'azione o stabilisce il criterio omogeneo di calcolo per la liquidazione di dette somme. In caso

class actions have been presented, none of them concerning insurance companies but some proposals for class action against insurers in on the way.[160]

§2. MEDIATION

477. In March 2010 the government approved a legislative decree to implement the EU Mediation Directive (2008/52/EC). Legislative Decree 28/2010 introduced a compulsory mediation stage for resolving civil and commercial disputes.

The decree's ambitious aim is to reduce the number of cases pending before the Italian courts and thereby cut the duration of a typical lawsuit – at present, the average period from the beginning of a first instance claim to the issuance of a final judgment by the Supreme Court is approximately eight years.

The Decree identifies the matter sin which preliminary mediation is compulsory in order to address in a second stage the courts: they include disputes involving property rights; division of assets; succession and inheritance; family agreements; disagreements between landlords and tenants; loans; firm tenancy; medical malpractice; defamatory statements in the media; or insurance, banking or other financial contracts.

---

di accoglimento di un'azione di classe proposta nei confronti di gestori di servizi pubblici o di pubblica utilità, il tribunale tiene conto di quanto riconosciuto in favore degli utenti e dei consumatori danneggiati nelle relative carte dei servizi eventualmente emanate. La sentenza diviene esecutiva decorsi centottanta giorni dalla pubblicazione. I pagamenti delle somme dovute effettuati durante tale periodo sono esenti da ogni diritto e incremento, anche per gli accessori di legge maturati dopo la pubblicazione della sentenza.

13. La corte d'appello, richiesta dei provvedimenti di cui all'articolo 283 del codice di procedura civile, tiene altresì conto dell'entità complessiva della somma gravante sul debitore, del numero dei creditori, nonché delle connesse difficoltà di ripetizione in caso di accoglimento del gravame. La corte può comunque disporre che, fino al passaggio in giudicato della sentenza, la somma complessivamente dovuta dal debitore sia depositata e resti vincolata nelle forme ritenute più opportune.

14. La sentenza che definisce il giudizio fa stato anche nei confronti degli aderenti. È fatta salva l'azione individuale dei soggetti che non aderiscono all'azione collettiva. Non sono proponibili ulteriori azioni di classe per i medesimi fatti e nei confronti della stessa impresa dopo la scadenza del termine per l'adesione assegnato dal giudice ai sensi del comma 9. Quelle proposte entro detto termine sono riunite d'ufficio se pendenti davanti allo stesso tribunale; altrimenti il giudice successivamente adìto ordina la cancellazione della causa dal ruolo, assegnando un termine perentorio non superiore a sessanta giorni per la riassunzione davanti al primo giudice.

15. Le rinunce e le transazioni intervenute tra le parti non pregiudicano i diritti degli aderenti che non vi hanno espressamente consentito. Gli stessi diritti sono fatti salvi anche nei casi di estinzione del giudizio o di chiusura anticipata del processo".

160. Le disposizioni dell'articolo 140*bis* del codice del consumo, di cui al decreto legislativo 6 settembre 2005, n. 206, come sostituito dal comma 1 del presente articolo, si applicano agli illeciti compiuti successivamente alla data di entrata in vigore della presente legge."

Index

The numbers here refers to paragraph numbers.

Index